Swallow Dance
A Collection of Poetry Chapbooks

Swallow Dance

A COLLECTION OF POETRY CHAPBOOKS

Edited by
Melanie Villines

Art by
Utagawa Hiroshige

SILVER BIRCH PRESS
LOS ANGELES, CALIFORNIA

© COPYRIGHT 2014, Silver Birch Press

ISBN-13: 978-0692235812

ISBN-10: 0692235817

Email: silver@silverbirchpress.com

Web: silverbirchpress.com

Blog: silverbirchpress.wordpress.com

Cover Image: "Swallow Dance" by Utagawa Hiroshige

Interior art: Utagawa Hiroshige (1797-1858)

Mailing Address:
Silver Birch Press
P.O. Box 29458
Los Angeles, CA 90029

Note: Authors retain all rights to their collections. If you wish to contact one of the poets, send an email to silver@silverbirchpress.com and we will forward the message.

Contents

JOHN BRANTINGHAM, *Lightning Storm* / 7-23

KIRSTEN DIERKING, *All Other Time Is Peace* / 25-41

PAUL FERICANO, *The Hollywood Catechism* / 43-63

CHRIS FORHAN, *Bone Box* / 65-77

JEFFREY GRAESSLEY, *Her Blue Dress* / 79-99

DONNA HILBERT, *The Democracy of Carbon* / 101-121

RUTH MOON KEMPHER, *Beach House* / 123-133

STEVEN KUHN, *Four Years in Pocket Change* / 135-155

TAMARA MADISON, *Out of the Earth* / 157-177

CATFISH MCDARIS, *Aida* / 179-197

CAROLYN MILLER, *In the Garden* / 199-211

JOAN JOBE SMITH, *Where the Stars at Night Are Big & Bright* / 213-225

RICK SMITH, *Letting Go of Ashes* / 227-247

FRED VOSS, *Wasn't Columbus a Bachelor?* / 249-270

About the Authors / 271

Acknowledgments / 275

Lightning Storm

John Brantingham

A Man Stepping into a River

A man stepping into a river watches the ripple of his foot dissipate away into the waters, and he thinks about all those poems and songs that talk about impermanence, and he is tempted for a moment to become maudlin and existential about the way time washes away everything, but the truth is that his foot did make an impression, his print was there, and just for a second, even running water was perfectly etched in his image and showed that he existed, that he was there, that he had done something.

Sequoia National Park, 1987

The first time I missed church on purpose
I was backpacking by myself,
had told Mom and Dad I would drive down
to the local church and look God
straight in the eucharist and talk to Him.

The first time I missed church on purpose,
I spent the afternoon under redwood trees,
teenage poor and arguing
with my phantom parents about God
and the nation
and backing up points
with Friedrich Nietzsche and Karl Marx.

The parents of my imagination walked
the forest paths with me. At first, they yelled
but eventually they were quieted
by the logic and purity of my arguments.
They listened and paused on our walk
to ask questions. They gazed upwards
as if to see the blue of the sky for the first time
in their lives. Eventually they were silent.
My father smiled at a secret joke
and shook his head slowly at himself.

The first time I missed church on purpose,
I waited until my daydream parents walked away,
and then I leaned back and talked directly to God.
I asked him all those things I had been
dying to ask him all my life,
and I waited a full Mass hour to hear
if he would respond.

San Dimas 1987

In cross country practice, we had the strange
ritual of wrapping shirts around our heads to stop the worst
of the sweat stinging our eyes and we'd arrange
our course so we'd be able to sprint in a burst
of masculinity past the girls' locker room
just as cheerleading let out.

We twenty young men without an ounce
of fat, thinking that this pulsating
run was what manhood was, that this flesh
browning in the smog-alert afternoon
was what we'd do every day and all the time
when we left high school for the real life outside.

Thoughts While Watching Kids Shrieking in a Fountain

Every kid shrieks when running
through a fountain, a hot day
and they get blasted by a jet of cold.
The kids this afternoon run in and out
of the water splashing each other,
each one thrilled that his stomach
can be so cold when everything
else blisters in the sun.

I try to imagine Hitler as a child
dancing in an Austrian fountain,
smiling, laughing in the spray.
I wonder if he splashed the girl who
lived next door as he half smiled
at her downturned eyes.

I wonder how Custer played
in the sandy swimming holes near his house,
if he would dive after the spoons
his laughing father would toss in
for him to find.

And I think about Gandhi
—when all the kids laughed and teased
the little boy who could not swim,
did he prostrate himself before the mocking
hordes to show them that he would not join in?

A Sestina about Fathers and Sons and Deserts and the Leonids Meteor Shower and How All Those Things Come Together to Show Us that Dreamers Like Me Absolutely Need Practical People Like My Father and I Try Not to Be Condescending as I Do It, but I Might Fail a Little

Novembers and we'd go out to the desert
to see the Leonids shower
in the cold
fall
nights. We'd drive way
out there where there weren't

any blinding lights like there are
in the city. I'd walk out past the edge of my parents'
conversation where the desert
started to turn frightening, way
out where I could tune out their voices and tune in the shower
thinking that one of the meteors could fall
right at my feet. It was the cold

dark out there, lit only by the cold
light of Dad's flashlight back by the car. He was
watching me, I suppose, making sure I didn't fall
into some deep desert
gully while my head was turned up to see the shower.
He knew the way

I got (and get) lost in myself, the way
I lose perspective on everything all around me, how I could
wander off in the cold
desert because I was thinking about meteor showers
instead of where I was.
    ➤

The desert
is a terrible place for people like me who fall
into a trace of daydreams, who fall
into thinking about everything else besides where we are. He knew the way
I could be lost in the desert
unless he kept his eyes on me as he talked to his wife in the cold. The way he saw it, I suppose, was
that he was there to take me to watch the shower,

there to make sure that I didn't die during the shower
that I didn't fall
to my death, but it was
up to me to figure out the universe for myself, figure out the Milky Way
and the Earth. It was up to me to be the dreamer, and he would stay the cold
numbers man he always had been. The desert

is about practicalities after all sometimes. In the desert, some of us see showers
and others have to be cold because that's the way
dreamers (who fall to their deaths all too often) force them to be.

Summer, 1982

I held back a bit,
left my legs mumbling
in the grasses
just a moment too long,
so when the baseball
arched out of the sky
I could dive head first
into the catch.

I waited for the cheers
of my friends
in a moment
that was silent
except for the sound
of a passing car,
except for the sound
of the Rainbird's click.

The *Trail to Bearpaw Meadow, Sequoia National Park, 1978*

The rhythm of my parents' footsteps and conversation dreams me into my own world as I follow them first by three feet and then by seven. Finally, I stop on the trail to hear what it's like to listen to their conversation disappear into the trees as they thread their way on.

The Trail to Bearpaw Meadow, Sequoia National Park, 1985

Summer pushes the scent out of the pines and soon, I find myself stumbling along the trail. At a creek I veer off the trail and uphill until I lie down on a great granite face. I wake up to the whooshing of a warm breeze through ferns. Nearby a coyote grooms himself, but we haven't seen each other yet.

The Trail to Bearpaw Meadow, Sequoia National Park, 2005

The rhythm of footsteps and a conversation wakes me out of my walking dream, and I can hear a group threading its way through the trees towards me. I could walk uphill to let them by and stay in the bubble of my world. Instead I pause and step off the trail. When they pass by, I smile and talk to them in the same way I do when I love people.

Starbucks on a Saturday Night

The couple in front of me explores each other's faces with fingers, palms, and lips, the way that only 15-year-olds can. Then they glance at me to gauge my shock. Their love is defined by the defiance of old men, so the third time they turn their hopeful eyes to me, I glower them into a rebellion of passion that they will never be able to feel just in the same way ever again.

Meditations on a Lightning Storm that Happened in 1894

My great grandfather, who neither I nor my father nor my grandfather ever met, died one night from a single bolt as he tramped across Ohio farmland. Just before the moment, he sighted a light in the upstairs window of his home, and his breath tripped a little in its joy. Inside sat his wife, pregnant with the new child patriarch, the child who died of old age 50 years ago this evening.

God Save the Queen

Halfway through a week of giving readings up here in tiny Canadian towns, my buddy Anders sets me up with a reading in a VFW hall. Knowing me, he tells me that there will be a picture of Queen Elizabeth on the stage behind me and that whatever I do, I should not, under any circumstances make fun of her or make any joke whatsoever. And it's a good thing that Anders knows me that well because the moment I'm on stage with poor Liz looking at me with those sad eyes that have lived through world wars and divorces and tragedies and depression and anarchy and the complete change of her culture, the moment I see all of that in her tightly closed lips, I almost turn around and go on a rant that starts with me being glad that my forebear got out of that foggy little island and ends with me questioning her gender. Of course, none of it would be serious—I have nothing but respect for the old woman who did so much. And turning around to see the faces in the VFW, I am so glad Anders told me what to do. I am surrounded by people who lived through those wars and divorces and tragedies and depression and anarchy with her. I am surrounded by people who believed enough in her to sacrifice money and time and personal goals, and they did it all because she asked, and because she suffered quietly with them and for them. So I do not make fun of her or these people. I show the reverence that she and they so richly deserve, and from now on I will say "God Save the Queen" and "God Save her People" and "God Save Canada" and "God Save All of Us" who need a queen, who would like a queen, who would feel just that much more secure in ourselves and what we were doing if she would step to the edge of her balcony, wave that little wave, and let us know that we were all in this mad, chaotic gumbo together.

Stopping at a Target in New York

The Targets in upstate New York are no different from the Targets in Los Angeles. They are the same nationwide, 3000 miles of conformity and comfort. And where you would find toilet paper in a beautiful quilted stack in Nashville, you will find that same stack in Seattle. The music is the same, the coffee is the same, and the same people stock shelves and smile at you from behind their red vests. It's no surprise that coming into this Target with Anders, I run into myself, the me that would have been if I had not moved to California when I was a kid. We're both there, me and my other self—me with Anders—my other self with those kids who would have been mine, a boy and a girl who are dumpy and not too bright, but who he loves in his own way. This is his life, these children he brings in here on a weekday afternoon looking for whatever tennis shoes that he can afford. He's become vague, whether it is from his home life or his job, teaching at a high school or working with the forestry service, coming home to his wife who's not quite sure she loves him but becomes suddenly terrified when she imagines him leaving her. He sees me and knows me, and he aches instantly for the life that I have, middle class, childless, with a woman that I love and a job that I love in a city that I tolerate. I look at him and his kids and think that would have been all right, and I believe it for a while. It's no surprise though that we envy each other a little, me not satisfied with what I have here in this universe and him not satisfied in that universe—all of us disappointed in the possible universes that together we inhabit.

Lightning Storm

    I'm teaching class during a storm that's happening at the exact same time a solar flare is arcing off the sun on an afternoon when four planets plus Pluto are aligned, and I'm into a long discussion of metaphysics when I sneeze just as a lightning bolt passes over my head stretching all the way to my house three miles away, and in that moment back at home my dog sneezes, and for a moment, my soul is taken out of my body, and Archie's soul is taken out of his body, and we switch bodies, and, for a brief time, Archie gains human consciousness, and I gain dog consciousness, and we both start to bark.

    For in that one moment, Archie can see his whole life so far stretching behind him, and he sees a clock, and he gains that human understanding of what time is, and that he's had time and that time is moving ahead of him, but that time is something that comes and disappears, and that time is going to come and disappear, and that he's heading for something that smells a lot like the end of his time, and that he's going to end some day, that he's going to die—just fucking die—and he's never spoken English before, so he starts to bark at my students—he loses it and starts barking through my body, trying to make the words that tell them he wants to do something—he has to accomplish something—it all has to mean something in some kind of profound way and aside from taking nice walks and guarding my house from well-intentioned neighbors—he can't see that he's done all that much even though I keep telling him he's a good boy.

    He barks existentially about time and the past and his puppyhood and he barks religiously wondering if there's a dog god and if all dogs truly do go to heaven, and he barks about all the wasted time, time we could have been together, but we were filling up hours with chores and arguments and worries, and he barks about politics and the Sudan and health care and the state of the government and how Pluto is no longer a planet and the fact that we're laying off teachers and the Invisible Children and the fact that we've let all of this become so overwhelming in our heads that we push it all out. ➢

He barks about all of this and more until he's just barking and barking and then those barks turn into a scream a long howling scream that makes my students wonder what all of this means and how it relates to the class, and the scream turns into a realization that he can speak English, and he wants all the answers and maybe some of these wide-eyed young people have the answers, when he sneezes again and finds himself back in his body, and I find myself back in my body, my voice now hoarse from barking and screaming.

But Archie can still see it all. He understands it all from a human point of view and a dog point of view and he keeps on barking, keeps on trying to speak to my wife, who is in the living room on her haunches trying to tell him that it's just lightning and thunder, and that he's all right, but he can't take it so he goes into the backyard and tilts his head upwards calling out to Pluto letting all the dogs on Pluto know that he knows and he feels and he wishes they could have a planet instead of whatever it is that Pluto has become but that sometimes we don't get anything that we wanted—sometimes we just get that dash of knowledge that ruins the whole thing. He barks all of this at the sky until he is howling so loudly my wife can't tell the thunder from his barks anymore.

All Other Time Is Peace

Kirsten Dierking

In Early Evening

Everything
around the lake

assents to silence.
All birds

agreed to hush.
All feathers, all fur,

felted thick
with fading light.

The boat comes
to a gentle rest

on the blue cusp
of still water.

Take it with you,
this interlude,

the sweet middle eye
of the storm.

Northern Oracle

The aluminum prow scratches over
submerged vines, drifts through platters
of lily pads. I lean to the side,
rest my hand on the water, touch
the sky of unknowable swimmers
feeding beneath me.

Sometimes I think the future begins
at the bottom of lakes. The next day rising
toward sound and action and easier
breathing. Darkness wanting
the candor of daylight, the simple shapes
of high noon, the plain faces
with no shadows.

I watch for an omen, but three feet
down, the sun disappears into murk
and secrets. The waves are reading
the lines of my palm, but show only this:
tomorrow coming like shimmering scales,
like transient bones fanned into dazzling,
silver fins.

Kayak

Minnows flash
sudden shafts

of silver light,
frogs stutter

guttural vowels
along the shore,

you feel like life
will go on and on,

if not this heron's,
if not your own,

then all the essence
of everything

that gives this lake
its wilderness—

all the bones
that rustle along

the shore today,
all the fuel

for future flesh,
for new fish,

for perch, birch,
and the petaled cups

of water flowers,
and you, for once,
➤

moving without
difficulty

between the blues
of water and sky,

why not
rest your mouth,

let the words in which
you think too much

spill out and drift
to the bottom.

Mississippi

The water flows persistently
towards some kind of finishing point,

maybe as far as the glamour of
a distant sea, maybe only as far

as the muck and blowsy cattails
hidden behind the next bend.

It's late September, and the first
cold gust shivers downriver,

brushes across your bare arms
with a touch that feels

both commonplace and ominous,
like passing your hand

through a spider's web.
You think about sinking your fist

into the current and releasing what
you long to keep—this bright sun

on open water, or even just
this quiet hour—and letting it pass

away from you, as easy as that.
What is it like to float without

any resistance anywhere the world wants?
You slip into the sandy shallows,

plant your feet here, then here.
But the current only detours a moment

around your ankles, that flesh and bone
you're so very fond of, and flows on.

Border Lines

Lying below the last open window
of late fall. Leaves drifting against
the screen like papery moths.

The dog with a long, groaning exhale,
releases herself from vigilance. Patrick
turns over, laughs out loud again in his dream.

How much will I miss, closing my eyes?
In the dark, my body, laid out for sleeping,
looks insubstantial as chimney smoke.

Now, no alarm, just a sudden waking
in colder weather, the future at hand,
my dark hair dusted with snow.

Shoveling Snow

If day after day I was caught inside
this muffle and hush

I would notice how birches
move with a lovely hum of spirits,

how falling snow is a privacy
warm as the space for sleeping,

how radiant snow is a dream
like leaving behind the body

and rising into that luminous place
where sometimes you meet

the people you've lost. How
silver branches scrawl their names

in tangled script against the white.
How the curves and cheekbones

of all my loved ones appear
in the polished marble of drifts.

Deep Winter

Make the cold
a blanket that mutes

the demands of the world
a drape to diffuse

the distance between
your grasping hand

and all you think
you're reaching for.

Think of these days
as a trail of reindeer

crossing the tundra,
antlers branched

in sprays of bone
against the sky.

Don't ask where
they are heading.

Don't ask the ache
of snow to stop falling.

In February, Think of Mexico

Leave behind
the cold thoughts
you can't carry.

Move south
until you are
an orchid
or a pink hibiscus.

Be a bird
with indigo wings,
a lemon yellow
angelfish.

Be the surf
and then become
the rising tide
and set your burdens
down on shore;

the coral bones
and bits of shell
and husks of all
the bygone things.

Be the blue
sigh of the ocean
gently pulled
from land
by the moon.

The Animist

> "*In the beginning of things, men were animals and animals were men.*"
> —from an Algonquin tale

In April when
the ground inhales
the yellow sun
and the grass
is suddenly
sweet and green
and you find yourself
lying down
and rolling in it,
you admit an animal
lives inside you.

If that kind
of exuberant creature
exists within
your plain skin,
what is hiding
inside the tree,
what kind
of glorious spirit
lives inside
the wildflower?

Lilacs

On the day of my birth,
I bury my face in purple flowers
and breathe a scent so familiar,

I can't remember a childhood house
with lilac bushes, maybe it was
my mother who held the baby up

to the dense blossoms, maybe it was
my first pleasure, my mother whispering
breathe deep, it goes so fast.

Thunder

I.

In the first spring storm of the season,
my husband says *we forget half our life has thunder.*

II.

It is mostly the sound of distant misses
and missed misfortunes. The whole world

doing dangerous things, while we lie together
as if we were the world's first animal pack,

and feeling, just by virtue of our limbs touching
and just by being not alone, undamageable,

and the most hopeful sense of protection.

III.

We were in bed when lightning hit the house next door,
a vicious fire quickly licking through the roof,

how trained we were from television to repeat the proper
platitudes to the uninjured but newly homeless.

Later that day, our tongues still thick with the taste
of ash and watered smoke, our talk hummed with a hint

of excitement, even triumph, that we had been so close
to danger and the strike had fallen somewhere else.

IV.

She looked through the picture window
of her new house, this house standing

precisely where the first one had stood,
and the window looks on the same scene—

empty park, lake filling with August weeds,
and she said *the view looks unfamiliar*

when you know the world can erupt in fire
at any time, at any given explosive moment.

V.

An old oak lies between two living trees,
no trace of the long ago lightning strike

that split the trunk, just this tender,
softening wood, and sheltered inside

maybe a small animal or two. I think
I would like to lie like that, spent body

waiting for cover and all the love
of the coming snow.

VI.

I open the window to a storm coming,
the thick electric humidity, the static

standing-on-end of leaves, the trees
and grass rapacious for reaching

ever upwards, ever anxious to further
entwine their roots and greens, ardent

always for more moisture to make
more and more of themselves,

and it comes now, not gently,
but with all the deluge of passion.

VII.

In the basement, under the stairs,
curled around the quivering dog,

clothes wet with the sweat of knowing
life sometimes depends on luck,

the howling wind drowns the shake
of the rattling house and masks

the crack of two great pines as they
crash in the yard, just a few feet away.

VIII.

There are few worse sounds in summer
than the searing wail of tornado sirens.

Yet look how easily we forget
what drives us into the basement

as soon as the season begins to change.
Memory is sometimes kind, and given time, ➤

you often can put losses behind you.
And yet, this same forgetfulness

must be what keeps us starting wars,
each generation the fresh launch

of a raw season, as if we had not
cowered in shelters, as if it had not

thundered before.

IX.

Hobbes said humanity is always prone
to fighting wars, but if prevented,

all other time is peace.

X.

If only half our life has thunder,
think of all the peaceable parts.

The hush of snow in the early
morning as you twine your fingers

through white sheets and into
the open hand of your partner

and remember you have hours before
there is anywhere or anyone else

you need to be. *All other time is peace.*
The clouds hold together seamlessly.

The Hollywood Catechism

Paul Fericano

For Kate and Greg Kelly

The Sign of the Double Cross

In the name of the Bogart,
and of the Cagney,
and of the Holy Edward G.
Amen, see?

Thank You, Elizabeth Taylor

for surviving the Hollywood
under your nails
all those Eddie Fisher records
skipping in your head
the Richard Burton years
echoing in your best screams
the uncorked bottles
the pills by the nightstand
the excessive weight
the plastic surgery
the heavy makeup
the chicken bone in your throat
thank you for not dying
for not being destroyed
by those two Oscars
a comedian's joke
your husband's campaign lies
and for telling the world
that Laurence Harvey
was your dearest friend
when nobody else could stand him

thank you for making distinctions
for not committing suicide
when everyone was writing poems
to a dead Marilyn Monroe

Moe Meets Freud in a Cigar Ship

Moe stands at one end of the counter
puffing on a pipe full of *Prince Albert*

blowing smoke rings
big enough to drive his *Studebaker* through.

Freud stands at the other end
puffing on a giant *Corona-Corona*

watching the smoke spin above his head
like a recurring dream.

This is not a place for talking or joking.
It's a place for quiet smoldering

where the cloud between the two men
is as thick as a couch, as thin as a gag.

Freud plays with his cigar now.
He strokes it, rolls it, turns it over,

slides it slowly between his fingers
then shoots Moe a knowing glance.

Moe stares past him with comic eyes
searching his slapstick brain

for one devastating wisecrack
that can drip from his lips like sap.

Instead, he says nothing.
He just puffs on his pipe and winks at Freud.

Freud pretends it's all in good fun
but moves away from the counter, just in case.

Chico Marx Explains Opera

Sure, I listen to opera.
I watch opera all the time on TV.
She's got a magazine, too.
But I don't read so good.

Prayer of the Talking Head

Lord, make me an instrument of my baloney;
Where there is truth, let me speak hokum;
where there is logic, twaddle;
where there is fact, drivel;
where there is sense, gabble;
where there is intellect, bunkum;
and where there is reason, mumbo jumbo.

O Divine Master,
grant that I may not so much speak
to be flabbergasted, as to flabbergast;
to be flummoxed, as to flummox;
to be flimflammed, as to flimflam.
For it is in jabbering that we jabber,
it is in blabbering that we are blabbered,
and it is in gibberish that we are born to eternal hooey.

Sinatra, Sinatra

Sexual reference:
A protruding sinatra
is often laughed at by serious women.

Medical procedure:
A malignant sinatra
must be cut out by a skilled surgeon.

Violent persuasion:
A sawed-off sinatra
is a dangerous weapon at close range.

Congressional question:
Do you deny the charge of ever being
involved in organized sinatra?

Prepared statement:
Kiss my sinatra.
Blow it out your sinatra.

Financial question:
Will supply-side sinatra halt inflation?

Empty expression:
The sinatra stops here.
The sinatra is quicker than the eye.

Strategic question:
Do you think it's possible to win
a limited nuclear sinatra?

Stupid assertion:
Eat sinatra.
Hail Mary full of sinatra.
➤

Serious reflection:
Sinatra this, sinatra that.
Sinatra do, sinatra don't.
Sinatra come, sinatra go.
There's no sinatra like show sinatra.

Historical question:
Is the poet who wrote this poem
still alive?

Biblical fact:
Man does not live by sinatra alone.

The Three Stooges at a Hollywood Party

The Three Stooges
get an invitation
to a big party
at John Wayne's house
but besides the Stooges
the only people
who show up are
Randolph Scott
Stuart Whitman
and Glen Campbell
who all drop acid
and beat the shit
out of John Wayne
just for the hell of it

John Wayne looks
to the Stooges for help
but they're too busy
melting down his Oscar

The Actor's Creed

I believe in Brando,
the Godfather of enormous weight,
creator of mumbling and angst,
and in James Dean, his only ward, our Jim,
who was sold into celluloid by Jack Warner,
born of the hustler Strasberg,
suffered under Rock Hudson,
was speeding, died, and nominated;
descended into gossip hell;
and on his third film was chosen
again from the dead;
ascended into *Giant* heaven,
and is seated in a bathhouse with Brando
the Godfather of enormous weight;
from where he will come to judge
all performances.

I believe in the Holy Spielberg,
the holy casting couch,
the communion of press agents,
the forgiveness of Sally Field,
the resurrection of my career,
and life everlasting without Tom Hanks.
Amen.

Dean Martin Talks About What's Bothering Him

When the moon hit my eye it had nothing to do with love at all.
For Christ's sake, what was I? A jukebox?

It was like a right-cross-left-hook combination I never saw coming.
I deserved it. I danced a little, showed some fancy footwork,

but after the first round, why bother? I dropped my guard completely.
I staggered along until I found the nerve to swagger.

When my voice buckled under the weight of my own jokes
I went down like the drunk I pretended to be.

After that whenever the moon took a swipe at me I learned to duck.
I got so good I could make out and make the bed at the same time.

Not so with those other chumps. We were all paying our dues
in those days. It was a living. You sang what they told you to sing.

But some guys believed their own press. They'd shoot themselves
in the head and expect someone else to drop dead.

Perry Como dreamt of Carolina moons so many times
he sleepwalked through most of the twentieth century.

Andy Williams kept drowning himself in a moon river
no wider than his own smile.

And Bing Crosby. There's a broken record that drove me nuts.
Moonlight becomes you? My ass.

As for Sinatra, he was the biggest sap of them all. When he flew
himself to the moon he dreamed he had wings on his *Guccis*.

Sure. Half the time I couldn't sing myself out of an empty casino.
But people got their nickel's worth. At least I showed up.

All this talk about the moon this and the moon that and the moon,
the moon, the moon. Let me tell you something: I hate pizza.

Frog Haiku
by Matsuo Basho

Translation by Porky Pig

Into the quiet of the anci-ancie-ancie—the very old pond
the small f-f-fro, f-f-fro-fro—er, the toad leaps.
The water sound is b-b-beau-b-b-beau-beau—oh, never mind.

Holy Cow, It's Moses

not really

it's just your strong
American memory
of all things Charlton Heston
commanding a reverent hush
in your Hollywood dream

listen:
one nation under God
indivisible like the Red Sea

Groucho Marx Throws Out the First Pitch

As the familiar strains of *Tosca* repeat themselves tonight,
take a bicarbonate of soda and skip the first act entirely.
If you can't skip, try prancing.

All in all we feel certain you'll be thrilled and delighted
by Puccini's music, which should come as surprise
since we're actually presenting Verdi's *La traviata* instead.

Of course, for the second act we hope to revive Rossini
if we can sober him up and find out what he did with Mussorgsky.
We tried to locate Handel but all we found was a brass doorknocker.

And if Rossini can't play we've got Donizetti ondeck to pinch hit,
although it isn't likely he'll get on base
with Tinkers, Evers, and Chance roaming the orchestra pit.

Nevertheless, we feel we've got a strong lineup
with Stravinsky on the mound, Offenbach and Bizet in the outfield
and Wagner batting cleanup and doing the dishes.

In fact, we've got a good chance to win the pennant this year
if we can just stay away from the third act. It would have been
a different opera season altogether if we could have signed DiMaggio.

Curly Howard Misreads Edgar Allan Poe

The director yells *Cut!* and everyone on the set
is relieved to feel the weight of the day lifted
like a dark comedy of unscripted errors,
no one more thankful than Curly Howard
who retreats to his trailer for a quick smoke and a drink,
rubbing as he goes his shaved cue-ball head,
where once the hair grew so thick
he actually appeared handsome to women
who fought to run their fingers through it.

He's reminded now of the sacrifices he's made,
the punishment he endures at the on-screen hands
of his older brother, Moe, who lovingly calls him Babe,
the mixed emotions he feels with each conk on the head,
each slap of the face or fingers poked in bewildered eyes,
and all the bricks and bottles and picks and shovels
and falling pianos and entire buildings collapsing
down around him in heaps of lowbrow humor and pain
can't hide the desperation of his clownish art,
the dreary midnight in his laughter.

Sitting alone, the alcohol convinces him otherwise
and he imagines himself a student of serious literature,
finding wisdom in the works of Edgar Allan Poe,
reading tales of unspeakable horrors befalling others,
grateful for this small refuge of scholarly insight,
and he commits to memory poems of young love dying,
mourning loss in a small room, much like this one,
childlike and powerless to rescue the slipping away,
the black doom of wings waiting above the door,
and he reads as he rocks, repeats the line
Quoth the raven, "Nevermoe," over and over again,
until he knows it to be absolutely true.

The Halle Berry

Halle Berry,
fool of none,
the Oscar is with thee.
Blessed art thou among catwomen,
and blessed is the fruit
of thy loom, *Jockey*.

Holy Berry,
mother of Chuck,
root for us winners
now and at the hour
of our last stand.
X-men.

It's Not Enough of Elvis

it's just not enough
it's not enough of Elvis whiskey decanters
Elvis toilet paper
Elvis condoms
Elvis impersonators singing Elvis songs
to Elvis fans
Elvis albums pitched on Elvis TV sets
to Elvis moonies
Elvis Cadillacs that travel Elvis highways
Elvis socks that fill Elvis shoes
Elvis snow skis with matching Elvis parkas
Elvis pillboxes stuffed with Elvis drugs
for Christ's sake it's just not enough
not enough of Elvis handguns
good-luck stick pins
disposable douche bags
golf balls
garage door openers
hideaway beds
and even poems like this that make you tired
it's not enough of Elvis
it's just not enough

we dig up the grave
and sell little envelopes of Elvis plots
we pulverize the casket
and market little vials of Elvis coffins
we auction off the corpse
and sell every last bone to the highest bidder
there's an Elvis foot
there's an Elvis foot without the Elvis toes
an Elvis collarbone
an Elvis spine jawbone ribcage finger
an Elvis thumb with part of an Elvis thumbnail
and of course there's an Elvis pelvis
➤

fetching the highest price in modern history
for a single work of art
and still it's not enough of Elvis
it's just not enough
we don't have enough
we can't get enough
and we won't rest until we've had enough

The Art of Quoting Harpo Marx

Like right speech, it should be practiced with restraint,
usually, when you don't have anything helpful to say,

about children, opera, or anything else for that matter.
And besides, no one asked for your opinion, anyway.

The Director's Prayer

Our Fellini
who Art in Carney,
Clooney be thy name.
Thy King be Kong,
thy Penn be Sean,
in Bert as it is in Ernie.

Give us our way
with Doris Day,
and forgive us
our Joan Crawfords,
as we forgive Eddie
for leaving Debbie,
and lead us not
into Snake Canyon,
but deliver us from Evel
Knievel.

Cut.

My Life in a Coma

I'm at the Academy Awards ceremony
sitting at a table
with Edgar Allan Poe, Walt Whitman
and Mrs. McBain, my fifth grade teacher
who starts writing on my dinner napkin in red ink:
"*Read more . . .*"

When I hear my name announced
as the winner of that year's *Best Supporting Poet*
and find myself being pushed out in the aisle
running towards the stage
and passing Leonard Nimoy
who's shaking everyone's hand for me.

When I finally reach the podium
to accept my Oscar from Rod McKuen,
Allen Ginsberg suddenly rushes out
from behind a curtain
grabs my Oscar
thanks a bewildered audience
and then races out a side door
where Lawrence Ferlinghetti is waiting
in a tan Ford Galaxy
with New York plates.

When I return to my table
everyone tries their best to console me.

Poe says that e.e. cummings
pulled the same stunt on T.S. Eliot years ago
diving through a closed window
and falling into an alley
where Wallace Stevens waited in a Chevy van.

➤

Whitman says he knows a place around the corner
where we can all get a sausage sandwich
and a whiskey
and meet some guy
who claims to be Carl Sandburg in drag.

And Mrs. McBain
finishes writing on my dinner napkin in red ink:
"Read more Emily Dickinson"

Morey Be

Morey be to the Amsterdam,
and to the Dick,
and to the Mary Tyler Moore.
As it was in the ratings,
is now, and ever shall be,
TV without Rose Marie.
Amen.

BONE BOX

Chris Forhan

Crude Articulation

From the word, the world: light, sky, squid, cancer
of the pancreas, Finland, Wallace Stevens, vocabulary tests.

God's stuck with us. God's in the word, in the word
made flesh. God wallows in the swamp of the body.

The saint is beholden to his calves and abdomen,
without which the arrows wouldn't wound him.

He'd have to fake that gaze of grateful yearning.
The Magdalene repents of the flesh. The flesh,

repenting of that repenting, persists in growing its hair:
russet cataract to her ankles. It's toil all right,

the heavy lifting and planting,
these skins we're issued erupting in boils

and itches, such a crude articulation are we—
erupting in beauty. We were bodiless once,

pure word. A word could unbody us.
Best not to be glib before the gallows

or to speak in our sleep. Best to dream
of scraping porch paint all morning, shirt stained with sweat,

of tossing the carcass of a bass into the trash.
Sleep is a parting. Best instead to wake

feeling that you didn't leave your life
in the night, that you might never leave it.

Aspirin and Shadow

Moon I swallow at dawn
to unsludge the blood,
haul it along: clump
of dust dissolving
that I might not
dissolve too soon

into this dust
I trudge across,
moonlight fashioning
a blackness I drag
behind me, long
blank flag of myself.

Petition

God of jaundice and cilantro, of laughter and catapults and
 spatters of duck shit on the train trestle, here is our want:
 what do you want with it?
Hunger, Lord, and love, more love than places to put it, this spit
 and ammunition, glut of coffins, glut of sunsets.
You who wheedled and scolded, then tore your tongue out,
 motioning meekly for someone to hammer a fat nail into
 your forehead, we said all we knew of you once, since then
 it's been twaddle and bosh.
God of the bomb in the hollowed-out Bible, God of the
 Forgiveness Project, of the jungle march at the tip of the
 bayonet, God of cabernet and sex and the Big Money Movie.
Our only begotten God, secret we whispered to the world, then
 forgot: come back.
Step from behind the curtain, appear as a boiling rain or flame
 or grumpy teenage girl, rejoin the quarrel, say something
 for yourself, say something and shut us up.

Third Grade

Our hands are folded before us on our desks.
Our hearts are bleached clean by contrition.
Sister Marie is standing in back of us. Her hair is hidden.
Our lunch pails are in the cloakroom. Our coats on hooks.
The alphabet is perfect. It smirks above the blackboard.
God is perfect. Our pictures of Him are tacked to the wall.
Bill is in his body, pale and gangly. Al is in his freckled body.
Delores is in her red-haired body. Phil, Kelly, Nate,
Erin in her thin, tall body. Jim, Sister Marie. My body
is in a white shirt, a little ink-blot on the pocket.
And outside: rain, iron, and silence.

Tattletale

I heard the world turn
its ear toward me
so I told what
my brother had done
and he vanished.
My mother
frowned, stopped
the faucet. Sweetness
drained from the milk
in my glass. The apple
on my plate halved
itself to bare
its white heart.
Suddenly, I had nothing
to say, stupid
in my body, hands
in my lap, feet
snug in sneakers—
dumb proud double knots—
my mind a sky
with a fleck of black in it
flapping in place.

Dream: Obedience

Some boys won't go willingly. I will.
Factory big as a city. Rows

of workers—innumerable, gray, eyes
down, hands busy. Far-off walls

of brick, grimed windows, grind and click
of gears above us. We're assembling

something we'll never see. A piece of it
lies in my palm, heft of a dead bird.

Someone among us is a traitor.
I walk past the camera, slowing

to show it my face and hands, to show
that I do what I don't understand.

While Reading The Lives of the Saints *in a Lawn Chair*

Flummoxed squirrel
scuffling up a tree
to the top, throat
screaking like a rusted
pump—he's caught
in the rapids of the river
flowing upward toward
whoever arranged this: I'd
like to stay
stupid a little longer please
about your purpose.

Nothing to It

My mind a lake of milk: a lack
of after, of before—all song

fallen from the ear, astonishment
gone small in me, a trinket

jingling in my sleep. Smirkless
face, past quotation. Grave's

taste fading on the tongue,
then hardtack, then nothing,

then one brushstroke betokens me.
No predicate. Weightless

as a page erased. And a sprig
of timothy for devastation.

Industrial Gothic

What we motored past to arrive
at this meadow, this light, this dew
cooling our feet before steaming
into oblivion in the June sun—

what we saw at dusk, smutting
the sky: the rust-glutted ironworks,
tanks and stacks and scuttles, cathedral
of fetor and soot, self-blessed
by waste: a bilious stew
oozing from boilers into grated drains
(whose ghost stokes the flames?)—
factory smelting beauty
to a rancid slag, the stench of which
we can't burn from our brains,

we who imagined the place to begin with,
we who adore it and are desolate.

Inventory

Pig bones boiled down for lip gloss,
Cannery ratchet chewing a girl's hand off at the wrist,
Pleasure boats, shoulder to shoulder, rising in the locks,
Deer stepping tentatively across the superstore parking lot,
Christ bullied out of his grave to paste disclaimers in
    high school science books,
Election day wins for witlessness, for swimming holes
    filled with shit,
And I, gazing at baby pictures, scribbling hymns a hamster
    would hear through tears.

Bone Box

I'm not dead so what do I know.
It's a box of bone I'm in. I work

the crash site, push glass bits
to the ditch with a broom.

A swift hit of spring
stuns me, but what's that.

My soul's not cracked in half
for its gold yet. It might be

bone in there, might be glass.
The glint of pearl, hint

of God in a swirl of snow
that's all the talk—I slowed,

made my brain blank,
did not blink, still missed it.

The Mother of Beauty

> "*Death is the mother of beauty*"–Wallace Stevens

I live on a planet spattered with blood and pray
to no patron saint. The risen Christ's a cloud—

can't swaddle him. In his mourning cloak, a butterfly
struts on the wind. At pond's edge, a heron

lifts from a rock and keeps low, gliding the riddle
of himself over the watery riddle beneath him.

A zero will swallow him soon, and swallow me.
Thus, his dazzle dazzles. Congress shall make no law

respecting that heron or my right to shift my ground
before I'm housed in it. I'm happy watching the moon

stay dead, its light stale and ecumenical. I am happy
enough. I am not lacking in happiness.

Her Blue Dress

Jeffrey Graessley

For Marlain

A *Constant Warrior*

dead space sound of paper
flicked across your thumb, waiting

for another morning to finish
growing and the white ghosts
of overcast to burn off.

the sun—a constant warrior.
you feel it fall upon your shoulders

reddening your neck
with that same oppression
that has marked all progression.
makes just getting up
a struggle.

stepping out your door
with sunlight branding challenge
in your eyes, yet somewhere
inside you
past that

dead space sound of paper
flicked across your thumb, waiting

lives a lion,
who raises his head
in rebellion

roars

and you endure.

And And And

wrestling with dead-memory
on a cold breeze, fighting
this numb sensation spreading
my skin, she's

a lack of feeling
in my chest, my heart
pounds that invalid sway
back and forth
of every emotionally damaged child
stuck in the system

the State says,
"no, no this one can be left
behind."

and bitterness
crawls up my neck,
like spider legs when
my blood warms

and her image dances
that one drunken time
to a two-piece band
down from Canada,

and in that memory
I realize
I hardly ever
check my phone
anymore

and I know
she needs her space
to march the San Bernardino
➤

ghettos, conquering new side
streets and gutters, collecting
smiles and catcalls
like pocket change

she'll have all the space
and time
and emptiness
she needs searching
the corners of her bedroom
or someone else's

never noticing before
all the cracks
that run the walls, like
every love-crazed lover's
psyche, smashing

his head up against
the padding.

Skin

i'm drawing images of you in the condensation
laden days spent watching shadows elongate.
skin—every bottle names your abrasion

words i won't remember saying, i'll touch
the empty space on the bed, conjuring form
i'm drawing images of you in the condensation

frozen moments watching the sky rise without
blemish, last night's poison still twists inside
skin—every bottle names your abrasion

surrender—failed expectation, once something
always something, and only from memory
i'm drawing images of you in the condensation

grass where we've exchanged our chemicals
with the soil, known the sunlight on our
skin—every bottle names your abrasion

all the slow songs that suck the color out of
everyone's face that never consider rain.
i'm drawing images of you in the condensation
skin—every bottle names your abrasion

I Can Hear an Angel Singing

sharing a cigarette
outside the library, her
eyes low,
a little red-rimmed, our
hands touch
first reconciliation another
bad night, she

has a hard time
admitting problems, and I'm
mute to connections

always believing
our hands
together
would carry us beyond
every word

hissed
between drunken teeth.

into another morning
outside the library
I burn my fingers
on a cigarette
before going inside.

Wolf Wolf Wolf

it's that easy way you were able to walk
through the door, to your car, tearing flesh
out, optimistic, and smile, dragging those cinderblocks,

you said that the lines aren't enough, no matter
how many notebooks i send, because
it's that easy way you were able to walk

that, like a stuck pig, run through, kills me every time
i wake to miss you, in dreams cracked, pulled
out, optimistic, and smile, dragging those cinderblocks.

i rip at the sheets with overgrown nails, pleading
for your memories, like a caged bird begs sky
it's that easy way you were able to walk

that keeps me looking at green Civics; a cascade
of hair framing eyes, your wolf grin, forced
out, optimistic, and smile, dragging those cinderblocks

that you never believed in and couldn't weigh you down,
untangle your hair, it's not anything you ever said—
it's that easy way you were able to walk
out, optimistic, and smile, dragging those cinderblocks.

A Priest at Work

She'll burn you
like the Inquisition
her words set men on fire
citing
Righteous Indignation
delivering LAST RIGHTS
through a bullhorn
marching the circumference
of a mass grave lined
with her lovers,
still bleeding. She'll

burn you lying from the pulpit,
in the confession box.
A snake constricted
round the neck of Moses
to get her point across.

She's killing in the classroom
on a returned smile that can't
be avoided, and only

the blind
deaf
and dumb

can hope for salvation
from her words,
like the gospel
she'll burn you

in parody of good news.

Getting Along

i still sleep in the kite birthmark on her cheek
four dark spots, disconnected along olive skin
high, where wind is born, blind by her mystique

she wanders, lost in other people's gardens, nails
caked in soil, she smells it, smiles, takes her leave.
i still sleep in the kite birthmark on her cheek

imagining my fingers tracing the dots naming
each a word for beauty like the many names of god
high, where wind is born, blind by her mystique.

she lives hours from me now, some other town
like a state of mind, she wants to be alone, but
i still sleep in the kite birthmark on her cheek

and i make it a point not to tell her about my bed-
time patterns, or why my mind is always
high, where wind is born, blind by her mystique.

it's the minutes and months without her, and needing
a new calendar; seeing others and wanting none.
i still sleep in the kite birthmark on her cheek
high, where wind is born, blind by her mystique.

I Remember

the hushed classroom
of our meeting.
a lecture on dialogue, I saw
your unpainted fingernails
and hands upward,
your voice a soft melody of ability
ever of the old romantic masters
kissed by their sweetness

that turned bitter
as time slipped from seconds
into months
without the joy of your tongue
that made other women
taste of poison
laced each of their words toxic
like exposure to pesticide, I waited.

for seasons to skip by
like sunsets
found comfort in others,
never capable of calling them
lovers. I remember

seeing your eyes look into mine
on the first day of Spring semester,
wounded, like all of your nights
are long nights, and wondered
if you saw all the same watched minutes
slow spin empty
days away in my own, I waited
as we sat in another classroom, I remember
the first time I heard your name called,
➤

my heart doesn't pound
that hard anymore, but
like your smile, I remember
when it did.

I'll Miss You

as bar-time slow crawls
a dying elk dragging itself
into death, and the faces
and the beer
remind themselves
of each other

and being alone
is my only hand
left to play, so I
leave and always

I'll miss you most
on those quiet Sundays eating
every meal outside between
kisses and poetry
blue smoke and symphony

and you throwing
your head back in laughter
or kissing my cheek
while I read another.

From Memory

we were foreigners
on the college streets
of Claremont, sipping on
masked Tall Cans
that looked like energy drinks.

packed bowls in the alcoves
under dome lights brightening
educated, unblemished faces
that never stared
at our crazed eyes
for fear of conversation.

sprawled on a park bench
under trees, a pocket
outside the concrete city
we're used to.

months after
we stopped being we,
and started being just
you and I

driving through
these soft streets, again
not seeing any pain
in the gutters, where the schools
don't say much about failure
cold weather
or giving up in a motel room
with steel hiding under a pillow.

I'm not saying goodbye
to you, baby,
only to the *we*
that once walked these streets.

Blessed

jacaranda petals
blanket a narrow stretch
of highway.

along a metal
fence marking
an unnamed rise.

where so many purple hands
let go of mother's brown arms,

goodbye,

on the wind,

kisses.

i drive past
blessed with a few
of her children
dancing
against my glass.

Fall

even the leaves know
suicide in the fall
jumping free from Mother's
branches to unforgiving
asphalt, minor fractions

span networks of splinters
little sections drift away

on tar oceans
dancing feet above water
like Jesus without the answers
mostly mindless chatter

and laughter
end over end
on top of one another

line the gutters
close enough
to whisper stories
for a lifetime content
like Monsieur Meursault
to live in the memory
of a single day outside
in freedom

waiting
with necks
exposed
to the guillotine, sun
pressing heavy
against eyelids

the leaves know suicide
sharp as the hanging blade
before it drops.

Dark Brown Hair

heart too heavy to carry
now
I leave it at home

when I'm talking
to women, I'm imagining
only one, and when
others give me their lips
on faces
or boxes

I keep my eyes closed
sustaining the fantasy
of dark brown hair
that likes to be pulled

I touch them
the way she likes
to be touched

never really hearing
present moans of pleasure
if there are any.

I'm stuck on a sound bite
hitting repeat
in my mind, because

my heart stays home
now
that she isn't.

Well

I don't use
the pillow on the right
side of my bed, near
the window

where there is a small
stain upon the fabric
of the case

a reminder
of her face
mouth open
snores escape
in little wisps
of drool

oblivious to everything

in her perfect glory.

Watched Silence

"A little bit dies
in me every time,"
she says, frowning
holding a Bukowski
collection. "Is this mine?"

I lean forward, disturb
a stack of her clothes,
"Shit."

"It's okay."

I grab the folded pile,
right it, and on top
is her blue dress
made of soft cotton
that gripped her hips
like elastic, I smell
the fabric, while she looks
at me through water lily eyes
spilling over.

"I'm sorry."

she takes the Bukowski,
packs her green Civic,
lifts her arms up, a goodbye
I refuse, saying,
"Why? The little bit of me
in you
has died already."

and she drives off
taking the night
that stretches
into watched silence,
as headlights flash
through my window.
everyone
moving right along.

Empty Hours

i want you
barefoot
knocked up
in the kitchen
singing
all your favorite
love songs, watching
summer skies
circle overhead.

i want you
asleep
on the bed
with a book left
open somewhere
nearby. i want you

in the cold empty hours,
when the lights
go out, and only
the memory
of you here with me,
remains.

i want you
in the kitchen
humming
while your hands
wrinkle
in hot dish soap
water. i want you

here holding our child
within the grasp
of your hips,
➢

and your breath
to become the sweet
lullaby i sleep to,
and wake
to find you
singing
in the kitchen.

Blind

i've read a lifetime's worth of your letters
kept in a wooden box, found empty
and all of it expired last night, ashes forever

will stream on a breeze, fighting
the distance between us, words in a bottle.
i've read a lifetime's worth of your letters

and have nothing left but blind excitement
the pretty faces and boxes—a new muse, maybe
and all of it expired last night, ashes forever.

a spoiled gallon of milk down the sink, and my notebooks
smelled like sweet pork burning, vague smoke signals
i've read a lifetime's worth of your letters

and don't want anymore, so please stop randomly
calling me in those empty mornings waking alone,
and all of it, Pigeon, expired last night, ashes forever.

the sweet melody of you in my heart has fallen
quiet, no longer can your smile shut my eyes
i've read a lifetime's worth of your letters
and all of it expired last night, ashes forever.

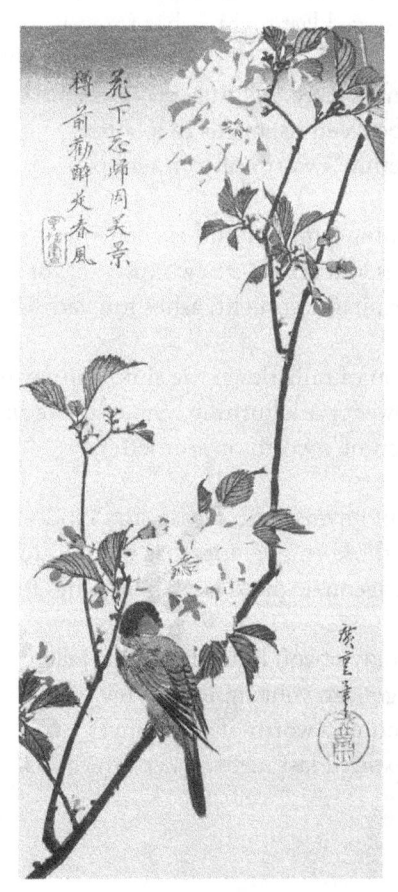

The Democracy of Carbon

Donna Hilbert

The Doctor Book

I loved the big doctor book
with cut-away pictures
of the human body,
the highway map of arteries
and veins, intestines
like the snakes I made with clay,
the liver, so slimy and dark
I could almost feel it slip through my hand.
Best of all, I liked the pictures
of the smallpox victims,
their bodies almost absent
under a mass of festering sores.
My grandpa had smallpox when he was a boy,
but recovered without a scar
to look like Gary Cooper.
If such a miracle were possible,
then surely I was safe in his house.

1942 Snapshot of My Father

He could be my child,
this boy at seventeen,
centered in front of a palm tree
in the parkway
of his sister's yard.
This motherless kid,

in a borrowed sports coat
and slacks that fold
too deeply over his shoes.
His curly hair is combed back.
His lips part in an almost grin.

I know the history of this picture:
how he came to California to find work.
How he dug ditches, riveted metal,
picked fruit,
returned to Oklahoma to marry his girl
before he turned eighteen. Nothing

to remark about, given the war.
And I know the life that followed:
the guns hidden in chimneys, bruises
under scarves, how the half-smile
concealed a boozy rage. Still,

it moves me:
how he glistens in this picture,
the deep crease of his slacks,
his boyish curls.

Mother in Satin

On Saturday nights, my mother

took off her blue jeans,
put on a red satin dress
with a wide circle skirt
that swished when she danced.

Or, a black brocade sheath dress
with a peplum of white lace
and rhinestone earrings
that jangled like ice cubes.

Or, to backyard parties, a pink
waffle piqué with a sewn-in
brassiere and laces up the back.

In springalator high heels,
open at the toe, she twirled
across the patio onto the grass,

unwinding like a bolt of organza,
her *Tabu* perfume simmering
in the torchlight, she danced

past the clothesline, past the built-in
barbecue, past the ornamental
fish pond, turning
into herself for the night.

Craving

I broke the long stems
of dry spaghetti
into worm-sized pieces
that I ate as I watched
cartoons on TV:
Baby Huey in his tiny diaper,
Porky and Petunia Pig.
I popped the round top
from the Hershey's chocolate can,
spooned the unsweetened
powder into my mouth.
Mom was pregnant.
At my eleventh birthday party,
Dad patted her belly,
bragged to my friends
that he'd *blown up that balloon.*
It was the beginning of summer.
My friends had begun to kiss boys,
steal candy and cigarettes
from Vons.
I spent the long afternoons
lying on the floor,
cartoons flickering silently
on the black and white TV,
the cord of the telephone
wrapped around my arm,
whispers of the high school boy
I knew from the park
slipping into my ear.
I ate the skin
from the tips of my fingers,
from the tops of my toes
until they bled.
I didn't know then
what was bitter,
as my life spilled out around me,
fine powder from a dark brown tin.

Madeleine

I think of you lying on the couch,
days after the birth of our boy—
your grandson—how your sobs
awakened me from fitful sleep
that first morning home.
You'd come to care for me, the baby,
your bewildered son.
Between the tears you said that no one loved you,
and now, surrounded by all this life,
you felt still more alone.
I watched you cry
as if watching a foreign movie,
in a language I couldn't speak.
I searched for meaning in what I saw:
your hair the color of bourbon
in the almost empty bottle
beside you on the floor.
I watched your face, still beautiful
un-mottled, smooth.
But I listened unmoved,
while you complained that I failed
to appreciate all you'd done—
marigolds planted by the back door,
the freshly laundered sheets.
Later, fueled by still more bourbon,
you started a fire
drying socks on the old gas stove.
I told your son to send you home
or I would take the baby and go.
Deep in my fertile life
I couldn't fathom such unhappiness,
didn't know the other meaning of passion,
had no language for such hunger,
had no language for such grief.

In the First Years

I don't know exactly what he does all day,
my fresh-pressed engineer
how his slide rule calculates
movement buried in the passageways
of pipes and tanks.
He uses words like
volatile, effluent, pressure.

But, I know what I do
rumpled mommy of two,
in a neighborhood so strange
I think it dangerous to stroll them to the park
alone. Mostly, I stay home
and wash piles of laundry
I never sort or fold,
cook food that doesn't taste quite right,
although I won't admit
nothing's ever really good.

Sometimes I drive him to work
when I want the car to visit
my mother in the valley.
The refinery air is sulfurous
and thick, it makes the babies
in the backseat gag, get sick,
vomit with such force they splatter my back
with flecks of puke, so I never
come entirely clean.

We go back after dusk
to pick him up.
The air still stinks, but the tanks
light up like Christmas.
In a couple of years the plant explodes
leaving a coworker dead.
➢

And, I will throw a plate of spaghetti
a whisper from my husband's head.
But in the first years, no notion
of what comes after—
the fragile welds that held us
a match strike from disaster.

Queens

I loved the flat sassy
bodies of my paper dolls:
movie queens,
hands on hips,
lips in a frozen pout,
glamour pusses
in tab-on fur capes.
More, I loved cardboard
Dale Evans,
Queen of the Cowgirls,
in her fringed suede jacket
and high-strutting boots.
Days, she rode Buttermilk
roping outlaws with Roy.
At sundown,
when she clicked her spurs,
buttermilk biscuits popped
from her oven. She sopped
them in syrup,
fed them to Roy.
Dale never got sticky,
never dropped a crumb,
never wore an apron,
was never jealous of Trigger
who shared their bed
whinnying and snorting
till sun up.

Domestic Arts

I am a young mother
so bored staying home
I agree to play Bridge
with my neighbors,
who I suspect put up with me
to find a fourth to fill the table.

They are goddesses of domestic arts,
and between games hold forth
on finer points of decoupage, macramé
and the transformation of cans
into casseroles.

Still, I am smug
for I have gifts of my own:
precognitive dreams
and *gift of the phone*,
which I demonstrate by chanting
*Mother Mother Mother Dear
call me now while my friends are here,*
and when the phone rings
they are believers.

Because I love an audience,
I tell them my dreams:
how I see trash cans burning
the night before they burst in flame
behind my house,
how Papa's heart attack
awakens me from sleep.
How I knew the night before she labored
Jan's baby boy would be born dead.

Now the neighbors play three-handed games—
Pinochle, Euchre—
keep their children indoors,
cross against the light
when they see me coming.

City of Lakewood

I
City of Lakewood's
Orange-vested workers chop
jacarandas into stumps.
I see this as I exit the 605
driving east on Del Amo.
The trees strike-slip
the sidewalk with their roots.
I guess this the excuse
to hack the jacarandas
to the ground.
What, come June, will console
us on the gray gloom days
without the trees'
profligate purple gown?
But now, it's February.
I turn north on Bloomfield,
enter Cerritos, a newer town,
with parkways of pear trees
in winter white regalia
still years from bursting
concrete with their roots.

II
City of Lakewood
are you jealous of the tree
living in three worlds
at once?

City of Lakewood
do you fear the secret of the tree?
In the democracy of carbon
we are one.

III
City this is that doesn't love a tree.
City of Lakewood.
There is no lake here,
and soon, I fear, no wood.

Grief Becomes Me

You've never looked better,
my friends Edward and Neil
tell me and lean close
for a clearer view.
I know what they mean
and believe it's true,
the same way earth and sky
wash to a radiant clean
after relentless days of rain.
How you would present me
with pieces of sea glass
tumbled smooth
from journeying canyons
and rivers to the ocean
and back again
washing up at our feet—
bits of amber, green,
and the rarest stellar blue.
Everything pure and impure
has leached from the soil
of my face,
and in the corners of my eyes,
hard crystals form.

Lesson

A portion of ashes we buried,
the portion remaining to be scattered
sits on a shelf
in my office, the container swathed
in a flannel bag, like the bag
protecting your tuxedo shoes.
How handsome you were in formal clothes!
Strangers often asked if you were *someone*.
Should they ask for your autograph?
The irreducible things that make up a person—
ashes, bits of tooth and bone—
transform from one noun
into another.
Before your death, Dear Heart,
I didn't know
that physics and grammar
are the same sad subject:
the transformation of matter,
transforming what matters.

Joined

Our kitchen, winter Sunday
boys playing on the floor,
I'm drying breakfast dishes
when I have the vision:
four chairs in front of a store
on a street I never travel.
Four chairs that will complete
our chair-less dining room suite.
I drive into the vision
and they are there,
with the same turned legs,
the same dark wood
as our furniture at home.
And on the bottom of one seat:
1927, date in the same hand
as on the table, underneath.

Everything sundered
wants reuniting,
everything rent, to mend.
So, I am not amazed Dear Heart
that nightly you walk
from the occluded country
to rest awhile with me.
Are not we
who have born three sons,
more joined than chair and table
turned from a single tree?

Traveler

You come at night to say you're leaving,
have dreamed of freedom for so long.
And more, you love another—old familiar song.
I call for Mother in my grieving,
but in her own dream, she's not speaking.
The children, uninvolved, won't say you're wrong.
Our friends are not surprised, say don't prolong
the misery, the pain, by not accepting
that you're gone. Because I refuse to hear
the first time you say you really have to go,
you speak again, louder than before, and wear
a new love on your arm, gesture meant to show
you have no love for me—I must forbear.
The dead are even colder than we know.

Flowers

The Farmer's Market flowers
of a certain age sit on my kitchen counter
waiting for disposal, their fresher
sisters already placed in vases
around the house. Red gerbera daisies
bending at the neck, yellow and purple
tulips open and blowsy as roses.
(Think Melina Mercouri still sexy to the end.)
I can't bear to throw them out
though their stems are slimy
and the water stinks of ammonia.
They have a languorous grace
leaning over the lip of the vase
as if standing straight were too much
trouble. (Think hookers in a humid city.)
But, perhaps they're more like the women
I saw last week lunching at the food court
in the mall, wearing gauzy purple
dresses, flowing pants and tunics,
gray heads under floppy red hats,
laughing and happy as if celebrating
the end of fashion, the too-tight
girdle of good taste.

In Plowboy's Produce Market

I push my cart through Plowboy's produce market
gleaning this song for the first days of fall:

broccoli cauliflower cabbage kohlrabi

The price of red pepper is dropping.
Eggplant shines purple.
Bell pepper is green.

I watch an old couple choose string beans:
she fills their sack by handfuls. He frowns,
empties the bag back into the bin,
then turns each bean to the light
before dropping it in.

pattypan crook-neck pumpkin zucchini

A woman wearing a scarf tight at her chin
eats Thompson's seedless from the grape bin.

Tokay Exotic Muscat Red Flame

At the melons, a man in white shorts, skin brown
as russet potatoes, swings a cantaloupe into his cart.
I think I'm in love.

Winesap Pippin Golden Delicious
where last week there were plums.

Old man, kiss your wife.
Wash your face in the juice of ripe fruit.
Put beans into your sack without looking.
Old man, we're in Plowboys's
every bean is perfect, every bean is right.

Credo

I believe in the Tuesdays
and Wednesdays of life,
the tuna sandwich lunches
and TV after dinner.
I believe in coffee with hot milk
and peanut butter toast,
Rosé wine in summer
and Burgundy in winter.

I am not in love with holidays,
birthdays—nothing special—
and weekends are just days
numbered six and seven,
though my love
dozing over TV golf
while I work the Sunday puzzle
might be all I need of life
and all I ask of heaven.

Deshacer

I open the garage door
and our dog bounds free
across the street
disappearing down the alley,
her black form unmade
by the moonless night.
I panic, run in circles with the leash
but you calmly cross the street
calling her name.
Because she loves you
she lets you bring her home.

I won't repeat the dream
in which you leave me.
Let's just say I know the world,
how it alters in an instant,
that I awaken sick
in remorse and dread.
I can't face again the dinners
with other lonely women,
then late-night TV
until the dog and I can bear
to go to bed.

I don't need again to learn
the bitter lesson
that everything I love
is a flame between two fingers.

Mansions

Live oak on yellow hills, below them, young vines.

The neighbor's children chase quail across the browning grass.

This landscape, Kris says, invites fire.

In the kitchen, Margaret and Sharon, laughing. The thwack, thwack of their knives on the cutting board, making salad.

That night I dream again of a new house: tall archways, oak floors. I reach for blackberries from my window.

Another night, before, a stab of dreamless wonder shakes me from my sleep.

Once, in an unfamiliar ocean, I thought of swimming home, afraid of steady beauty: dark bodies against the pink-gray stone.

Or, that relief (rounding the corner in another car, seeing my car in the driveway) of already being home.

In this dwindling heat, I grow used to uneasy sleep, the terror of disinterested perfection:

scent of fennel, women laughing,

the burnt oak stately among the untouched trees.

What God Wants

> *God has given you this beautiful day, and what have you given God?*
> Man in front of Union Station, Los Angeles

I can't imagine God
wants a fatted calf.
Surely She knows better
than to feed on a fad
diet. As for sacrificing
firstborns, that's been
done to death.
Perhaps God would like
something in cashmere.
How about a Rolex?
Or bright yellow Hummer
that says *get out of my way!*
Maybe God is not
a glutton for consumption,
but an overworked
mother who wants a day off
to lie on the sofa,
sip Diet Coke and watch Oprah—
a little peace
and quiet for once.
Someone else to pick up the kids
and make dinner
while She soaks in the tub.
Then later, with everyone seated
around the same table,
She would like just one meal
where no one spills milk
or complains
about the food set before him,
no one kicks at her brother
or pinches his sister.
Just one meal
to be eaten in gratitude
to be eaten in peace,
is that too much to ask?
Is that too much to want?

The Angel Garmin

Long have I wished for a calm voice
pointing me home,
a confident voice telling which fork
in the forest road,
leads to the soup, the bread,
the welcoming bed,
and which to dead-end
doom instead.

One night I circled a flat Texas town
for hours in my rented Ford
searching for the Hampton Inn
I'd left in daylight before
the unpredicted storm blew down.
The water rose; the gas gauge fell.
I surely had foretasted hell
lost in the unfamiliar, flooded town.

Now, the Angel Garmin takes
me through the four-level interchange,
over cloverleaf and roundabout,
keep left, exit, turn right,
she tells me. Perfect
mother, guardian, guide
all knowing, but flexible, kind,
never scolding when I fail
to turn as I am told,
she simply *recalculates*
finds me, brings me back home.

BEACH HOUSE

Ruth Moon Kempher

Patience, I Tell Myself,
Is a Hard Virtue

as I count yellow flowers of weeds
white-spiked bells of the yucca

small fish flying
out of the surf, with deep

relentless shapes beneath them
swimming. Two turns into three

but without reason. *Lo que
me falta*—what I need

salt, this season.

Later, shadows of night
are caught in the bell-tips

in the yucca—Spanish Bayonet
they call it here—

hung on the undersides of leaves
as crickets signal

electric irritation, fence
to fence. All sanity

snaggles on a barb-wire prong.
Tomorrow the same. Or rain.

All overlong.

Fortune Teller

Seven tiger-tawny conch shells
and one stone, eroded to a worm's Rosetta
globular, like a pregnant woman's belly
rolled up on the beach.

I had asked for omens, but

surely the shell's shape
is of cornucopia, and the stone's expectant?
The signs seemed good, but like runes
or tarot cards, the beginning's

not for amateurs? Yes, but I believed it

and that's the problem—
joyriding on half a scad of isms
I cling to gone dreams, old yearnings
mull and muse over shells, and that stone.

Either everything has meaning or nothing does

hardly both ways.
Dream about doors, I do, and other
progressions, mirrors, and eggs.
Old stars crossed, web-wound, twinkled plaid
the night that I was born, I told you—

you with your cool hand
star in your palm, lines in grooves like crosspatch—
damp hand, like a soggy piece of toast
sweating pure butter.

I believe that, too.

Hands: Home After Bowling

I have watched
my hands age until
now, the veins are
gnarled, blue grape-
vines, risen—
have seen dishes
slip into sud-slops
washing up, and slit
one finger on an
envelope—

my stepfather
sending prayers and
greeting, remembers
my "golden-hearted"
mother, touches
my heart with words.
He is Turkish, has
other daughters
but he hasn't
forgotten, nor I.

Tonight at bowling
my hands faltered—
missed a split badly
dropped the ball
into the gutter—
but then, I remember
the same hands, younger,
gripped my mother's
at her bedside, slippery
with sweat, clamped
hard, did it—
hauled her home.

Arrangement, with Tiger Lilies

    Orange tiger lilies, with
magenta mums, and white cinnamon-scented
carnations in a funnel of green fern fronds—
see how the orange petals
dominate, drawing the eye to their sprawl.

    This is not
what you could call a still life. It is quite
a moving presentation: cut-off blossoms in water.
Singular flowers, surrounded by their modest neighbors
the lilies proudly display their sexuality.
Stamen. Anthers. Seed dust.
All upthrust.

They say Come, fertilize us.
We're open. We're willing. We can't run away.
But come quickly and catch us; see how we're fading.

Sad flowers. Reciting the story
of so many gone lovers
in their blue vase.

Toenail

   1:30 *a.m.*

Holding my toe
at an odd angle
in lamplight
  like some Zen person
    whacky from
late lawn raking
lost in contemplation
(bamboo pattern sheets
    no help)
"O," I said. "What a strange
old toe."

Bonnet of nailbone
on a weird creature face
    ribbon of dirt
smiling. "How?" I asked
reacting at first (in wonder)
at the lovely Georgia O'Keeffe
    antelope skull with
hollyhock eyehole. "It's
so real it's artificial?"

But no. Buddha in bamboo:
my toe is not so old.
It is simply
unshorn.

   A woman with a
regular gentleman caller
(for courtesy) trims
her nails proper.
   I have merely
lived too long
alone.

Tongues

> *It's all Latin for lonely.*
> Laurel Speer

A tongue is:
    a tactile O dear organ of touch and also
    sensual delight, as with whipped cream or
    those slushy things out of a machine, as
    unmechanical a limber creature as ever
    roamed if ever allowed loose on a summer's
    evening probably instrumental (as organ)
    in more communications of a wholly person-
    al nature than Adam's
& tongues are:
    not so simple. Speaking of speaking in
    tongues, here we have the universal rather
    than let's say we wonder about life or in
    that same crepuscular evening's lavender
    are searching for words like O dear a
    sudden magic in the air, O fireflies!
can mean so much, either way.
The word "tongue" derives from maybe the Latin-
ate *tangare*: to touch? Now I'll go look it up.
    There are 37 definitions of "tongue," up to
    & including a strip of leather in a shoe,
    a part used to harness oxen, none of which
    came to my mind when I started this.
    I started, thinking of you.
It comes from Old English. *Icel?*
I hear you whisper, "Cool."

Rutabagas

blue, like old linoleum
and peaches
with fuzz and smell of bees—
these sit on the counter, unconcerned
    as jazz
drifts over their textures, and fear
limps by, to the aspirin bottle overturned.

Sometimes vegetables, fruit—that's
the safest thing to be.

        Hazy at the Market

        green tomatoes

        forced in some flat
        or with neon sunshine

        not enough vitamins
        to nourish the blight

        wormless, of course
        worms appreciate taste

        why do I think of love
        in connection with

        packed in plastic, green
        tomatoes? why am I faced

        it is solid pulp and green
        someone I could trust

        vegetable connections
        dreams: soft rain

Driving Home on the Beach Road
Formulating a List of Things

with which to empathize: what I'm most like
is a rest stop in Georgia, on I-75 and then
how I'm something like a First Aid Station
bound for hurricane country and a storm
somewhere bustling up the coast
there's just folks stopping in
who bruised a finger, boarding up
    or stepped on a nail
pulled loose, but sooner or later
    not now, just
being sent home, to wait—
a competent small brick shack-up
    station or stop

'til later, still driving, listening
as the weather guy pants his forecasts
    crazy
glimpsed the Jax Beach Holiday Inn sign—
    pasted over
    and I'm like that thing, too
I thought, reading:

THIS SPACE
    AVAILABLE

    but what
I toyed with most of all was how
over the chill grey morning
smiled a cool, implacable slit
of crescent moon.

Conjure Lines—Sea Changes

as the sea's forever motion
rolls fish and shells, porpoise, whales
like an old gypsy fingering silver, the hours
      rearrange themselves—
turned surf, like whorls within a conch
grey, pale pink and orange, returns—
there's no hex strong enough to stop it, just
possibly echoes, little girl's laughter
as they build their castles.
              Watchful fish
    stand on their fins in wonder
as the old moon sails a quadrilateral orbit
like a broken platter, across cool morning sky

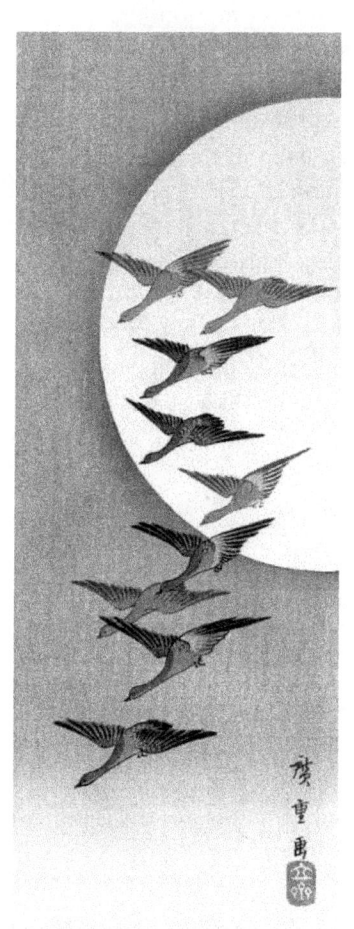

Four Years in Pocket Change

Steven Kuhn

Words, Movements, Pictures

Each word is a vision:
blue skies and oceans full of surging waves.
Each movement of the lip, each singular motion
is a staccato thought,
ripe with blood and living breath
and seems to suggest
newness. Freshness.
And despite our wishes well,
each word will cost
a thousand and one most precious coins of thought.

She is a broken cathedral,
pillars cracked,
vast and beautiful and distant.
Intoxicating . . .
In her cool airs,
in the smattering of violets that spring
from the most casual of her glances,
I find a moment's rest from thought.

In the quiet that follows,
I wonder if that is good enough.
If that is worth a mistake.

PART 1: Words

Word

I dreamt of a new word last night.
Refreshing, in 3 or 4 syllables:
   like "honeydewdrop,"
   or "applesnap,"
It was a joy to write on lined paper.

A perfect word, it encompassed something beautiful.
It popped like "apoplectic."
A dignified, but sweet fruit, like "aplomb."

It sat atop a poem,
the best I've ever written.
But 4 lines in, I suddenly knew that I slept,
and I wrote the word on my hand,
knowing that dreams fade on waking.

When I woke, there was nothing written on my hand.

Nothing to Say

An indifference blows like wind today
through alleys and crevasses,
through the narrow rock walls of canyons that stand
between myself and myself.

It stares me down,
silent, and not right,
or anyone, really.
His face is unfamiliar,
but I don't really feel like looking.

It blows careless,
tired and accepting,
in the space between our eyes and noses.
It sweeps up the connections that are made between people,
of purple and blue, even yellow—
understandings yearning to be made.
To be. To exist.
Pushed to the edges of the horizon,
they are clouds on a cloudless noon.

An indifference that blows like wind—
I can almost point to it, moving in the air around me.
A not-solid object. A depression of light.
A floating absence,
a living thing that breathes in my ear,
and is just out of sight as I turn my head.

In this stillness that the sun reaches out to me.
I will accept its embrace,
but I cannot listen to its speech.

I am an accident victim, wrapped in a blanket,
staring out the ambulance window
tuning out the paramedic's words.
" . . . it'll be alright, it'll be alright . . ."

My accident is myself, and the sun has no words for me.

Adam's Apple

A yellow apple, not gold,
Hangs on a snowy black bough
in a green field.
Not gold, the gold is hidden;
it is carried in the hard leather claws of birds
that migrate
in circular and cerebral patterns,
In strange variances of height.
Up and down, we swallow the Adam's apple.
It jogs forever in our throats,
never fully digested.

For . . .

This poem is for someone who does not exist—

Whom,
If they were to ask why there are so many question marks
in my notebook,
I would say to them,
Because art is like life.

When

And what are you to do then?
When
everything that held your attention for so long
kept your fancy
distracted you well
seems like dust
poisonous and denouncing
pouncing
like a cat indifferent to the catch
after the kill?

You can put on a sad song and sit
in the dark
and reflect on the way the moon looked on the water
and her silhouette throwing sparks
as she danced on the ocean—
raised both arms high,
and grabbed the ends of the sky with both hands
pulled it down to the water like a black tarp,
shimmering and sidereal,
filled with the wind.

The Two Fates

Choice lies broken
in the bottom of my book bag
like one more pair of cheap sunglasses.
Satisfied that Fate
is nothing more
than vicissitude.

Goodbye

A goodbye hovers in one corner of my mouth,
hiding behind an indifferent molar;
the kind of goodbye that pries an open smile through seething pain.
It is peeking down my throat at the prospect of starting over.
It is unsure of whether or not it should leave.

Between the Lines

hearts beat
blood flows
lovers meet
love grows
for ill, for treat,
we live in throes
love is sweet
until it goes.

PART 2: Movements

Defining the Girl

Waiting . . .
Little sadnesses float always apace behind her
perfect and silent spiders on thin webs
which everyone sees.
They think,
"my what glorious webs are attached to her"
but they never say it.

You must never talk about those hewn-glass
those crystal webs,
perfect and pure and brilliant: they were
dropped and shattered and left behind.
Broken diamond dust.
You must joke about something else
a little less
demanding, perhaps.

Waiting . . .
some people can spend their whole lives waiting.

And yes,
Life happens
to some of us.

My World

I am from a world . . .
of subtle charm
and . . .

Flash—

A man lighting a cigarette
in a car that drives away.

Riding a Greyhound at Night

Quiet hum and dark without,
ours is a vessel that is a world unto itself.

Anything but smooth, we speed as if in a tunnel.
The harsh grit grabs at tires that grind.
Always rolling,
they moan.
they howl.

Passing a semi, we drift mere inches from the trailer,
full-forward and swaying,
spitting dust and gravel eddying into its headlights.
It would be like watching a movie—
except for the scream of the wind between us.

The only light is occasional—
fluorescent-backed signs of dirty plastic that advertise
for businesses long closed.

Quiet hum and silence within—
A lingering and dreamless half-sleep.

15 or so passengers, 15 nameless faces. 15 silent battles with . . .
something or other.
What we each think, for the most part, is our own business.

All this dark and contemplation,
all this humming and swaying and shaking—
it's as if the light, the trembling coach, ourselves,
are being pulled through some dayless oblivion,
sunless purgatory,
toward an equally silent disembarking
ten thousand gas-station-and-fast-food towns away.

A Long Second

Sometimes life is like water
tracing slowly in smooth, cool droplets
down your fingers
to drop
delicately
onto purple velvet.

A Kiss Of . . .

A
kiss
of
long island iced tea
. . . just tastes the tip of my tongue.
Not near enough to burn.
Not near enough to intoxicate.
Penetrate
me
Break through like rocks
crushed to cinders
like life
like
love

Ether Touch

Ether touch, skin like milk
A velvet hand on a bed of silk
Or not a bed, but some ethereal couch
Where your head rests on my shoulder.

Lying quiet,
I feel your fingers tracing the imperfections of my skin
Lighting, a yet-unimagined insect,
on . . .
Everywhere you land your gentle sting,
I go numb
Smile,
Close my eyes.
I imagine my body sectioned off
into one foot diameter squares
Like one of those electronic memory games from when we were kids . . .
Dark, until you run your hand over,
Then brilliant with different colors-
lights behind cheap plastic—
Soul behind the dirt.

I imagine myself without skin,
A pond that you sit idly by, in summer,
Lying on the bank with your head propped up on one elbow,
Beautiful
as you carelessly make ripples
everywhere your fingers happen to land.

Midnight in a perfect world *

Midnight in a perfect world—
Light footsteps barely heard, even in the silence.
The daydwellers sleep,
Nod off in front of blue glows from television sets,
Or with their backs to their loved ones.

Midnight in a perfect world—
The imperfect can't sleep.
Walk the streets.
Move like phantoms, unnoticed, through a plane of black and yellow.
Streetlights. Blurred at the edges.
Turn up the collar, the wind cannot touch you.
Let it bite.

Midnight in a perfect world,
Drops of water on the windshield catch the headlights of a car speeding the other
direction.
Look in the rearview—
Red lines of taillights fade in the dark, and are gone.

Midnight in a perfect world.
Walk past the empty windows,
Darkened displays—
Sale. 50% off.
Everything must go.
Walk past the deserted spots,
The crackle of neon signs.
Walk past glass and concrete,
Stone and steel.
Look at your watch.
It's a quarter past midnight in a perfect world,
And I'm restless.

* *This title is from a song title that inspired the poem. Used with permission of the artist.*

PART 3: Pictures

Shutterbug

Her body moves like music
She sweetly spins
and scathes
in slow motion.
A slow staccato
Stutter
Click—snap the shutter
Cluttered—my feelings . . .
Fluttered,
Shuttered my heart . . .
I don't want to play by the rules anymore.

Antiquity

Ivy on stone walls
A park bench in the middle of a garden
On the grass.
Old churchyards with crooked headstones.

A faded smile on a dusty picture,
Lips and eyes bright with the security
that comes from a moment in hindsight.

Breadcrust

All I want now is stillness.

A cessation of the jingling change in the left pocket of my jeans
like so much broken glass.
A casual surrender to the night-noises in the lack left there
caused by the loud, the not-me.

It seems like such
a sin
Your breath still clinging
desperate and hopeless,
mostly just tired,
to my skin.

Bluish-monitor-TV-glow, a makeshift lamp
soft on your skin, your smell still in my hair,
The sight of your teddy bear knocked to the floor, I'd like to
    think.
But not knocked—
dropped quietly—
as if going through the motions.

It seems like such a sin
to crave only sleep
and maybe dreams penned by Eliot.
And at least now, it seems
like such a sin to keep trying.

Hangover Morning

Watching from a distance as friends
attempt to kill an afternoon
with volleys of bottle rockets.
A rapid push towards the sky,
A crack and a spark,
The final, terminal descent—
rain of thin red sticks and burnt paper.

Smiles beyond the headaches—
these are the lives we have chosen up to now.

It's nice to know that after the debacle and the sound,
You can still sit on a swing on a grey afternoon,
And reflect on the world's silence,
whether shocked or indifferent,
or simply silent,
masked over with distant laughter.

Joy

I stopped under a tree
At night during a rainstorm.
Drip,
Drop,
Down onto splashy stones.
Steps, strong,
Silent sentinels seeping . . .
sleeping?
As the drips
Drop.
Sounds like sighs,
They splash in the
stream below,
And lap at the leaves
loves
go by in my mind.
And still the drips
drop
in the lamplight.
Causes a haze,
a mist,
a beautiful, unbroken bliss,
benevolent, bursting,
as they break on the
bricks;
Wet like the backs of bottlenose dolphins—
without fins—
scoffin'
at the typical:
a tickled tirade toward those tired daydwellers,
who would run from the rain,
and miss
this
sweet
scene.
Drips
Drop
Down
Fall on my face.
I feel *alive*.

Subtle

I.
The rock and twist
of an oak leaf's fall
is gentle in the sway
but a fall nonetheless.

II.
. . . and what a sight.
Tree leaves shiver in the wind at night—
beneath a yellow streetlight.

Woman on a Plane

The woman on my left is reading a sad novel,
white handkerchief in hand,
bottom lip struggling to dam the tears
misting her pretty face.
They make her skin look like old glass—
dull shine and drooping—
thicker at the bottom than in the middle.

My Time

This is my time.
Right between midnight and
one.
Clouds low above my city,
not grey,
but dark black, low, and pale yellow.
Trapping light, and air, and thoughts—
holding for ransom
all the empty buildings and sleeping dreamers.

These are my people.
Fellow cross-carpenters and carriers all:
the night-shifters whispering over my shoulder,
smoking outside the 24-hour pharmacy,
brooding beneath the soft, fluorescent lights
of all-night coffee joints . . .
yeah . . .
breakfast served anytime . . .
Settling on plastic stools,
clinking money in the jukebox,
perusing the newspaper,
or talking, or smiling, staring,
or whatever . . .

This is my road.
Deserted white and yellow lines,
broken or solid,
rushing,
sliding beneath tires unseen,
unnoticed.

The soft fluorescent lights and the whispering,
the brooding and the buildings and the smoke
and the streetlights,
the
night
self-contained beneath clouds
that are dark black, low, and pale yellow . . .
And somewhere above,
There's a promise of stars.

Shine

Shine.
The only light on a dark night.
Thunder and ozone play soft on the senses, yes,
Soft
on the eyes, the nose, and the ears.

The feel of cool wet bark,
That stains your hands like charcoal and smells like life,
Is something primal and beautiful.

In the street, the shine makes a line.
An i, dotted by its streetlight source.

Light through wet leaves like paper,
Like photographs on a drying rack,
Each one is a memory, unique,
On the branches of your cerebral cortex.

Shine.
Picture the shine of a streetlight on wet spring branches.
Now what does it make you feel?
To me it's like slivers of white on a silhouette,
The world in noir,
Black-and-white film in motion,
Changing as it slides beneath your feet.

Out of the Earth

Tamara Madison

Lion Hills

From the pine-sharp spine
of California roads descend
to the quiet, muscled belly
where stone fruit grows
and low hills gather
like watchful cats
to rest
in yellow grass robes,
the velvet of lions.

In the golden undulation
I look for limbs—
haunch, foreleg,
fan of claws,
huge lion head
breathing low
the dry August wind.

In the hotel bed
our knees rise
like lions' limbs.
While the high moon
lights the blue-gold hills
with night
I will dream
of the earth's shiver
that created them,
the great lion souls
that sleep beneath.

Give Me Your Clouds

Give me your clouds
Your big clouds rising like cakes in the oven
Blue clouds heavy-bottomed, looming
High clouds scratched by wind
Clouds like a sun-bleached spine

I want white clouds billowing up
with a narrow sword-gray cloud
ripping through the middle
Clouds like cotton batting
Clouds like quilts
Wet clouds pulled apart by wind

I want steely clouds, pink clouds,
purple and apricot clouds
Clouds trooping like sheep
across a cool blue April sky
a puffy stray one
left behind by the herd
moving slowly away from the horizon

And I want shy clouds, too
Thin, modest clouds shaped
like a smile its wearer doesn't know is there
Little eyelash clouds
Clouds like silk cocoons
Sheer slips of clouds wisping across
a dragon's eye moon.

Kepler-22b

There you are at last!
I'm sure it's you—
I can almost see you
there, waving at me:
my twin, my soul mate
my lover. Now
I can give up my search.
It's only a matter of time
when we'll be together
my love, my perfect
love. At last
someone who sees me
who knows me
who understands me
without words,
someone whom I too
will see and understand—
someone I can devote
my life to.
It will not matter
that our arms
may not match
that our bodies
may not fit
that we have no
common language
but the language
of desire
pulsing from your heart
to mine
over the mere 600 light years
that lie in the vast
and hopeful darkness
between your balmy
juicy world
and mine.

To a Mortar

How sturdy you stand there, your body
of marble curved like a thick stone goblet,
black veins running like rivers along the arc
of your torso. Your maker has tattooed
your smooth inner belly with ridges
to ready you for your task, and given you
a mate: marbled, cool and smooth like you,
in a phallic shape scored rough at the head
to better do its work. But this is no coupling
of animals; your bowl is too wide for this tool.
But you are Eve, the pestle your Adam,
and the world is new to you both as you stand
at my kitchen altar, mute virgins: you poised
for the grinding, he prepared to pound. Today
I join you together in a marriage of garlic,
basil and pine nuts. May the fruit
of your labors bring to this table many
a fine meal, and the aromas of your work
fill this kitchen like the voices of a choir,
redolent with melody.

Baby Vegetables

I pry open the plastic clamshell
of baby arugula, tear into the bag
of baby lettuce, pick the baby carrots
from the market bin and tuck them
into my recyclable supermarket tote
with the other baby vegetables.
They will be delicious but still
I will feel like a pedophile
enjoying these sweet young flowers
of God's creation before they have grown
to full size, before they have basked
their intended amount in the sunlight
or slept enough in their earthen wombs,
before they have drunk their allotted share
of earthly water. Someone else
has cut short these tender lives and we,
my friend, are devouring them
like perverts in a damp garage.
And they taste so good.

Morning Glory

Grown
from leftover seeds
sown at the foot
of a shaky trellis,
an expert, you reach
that first rung
and climb daily
higher, wind
so surely
around
each post.
Your vines
will scale the top
of the trellis
and the brick fence
behind it; by then
you'll be showing
your velvet-blue funnels
but for now, I admire
how you rise
each day higher
twine so deftly
around the supports
to display your mass
of heart-shaped
leaves like a fall of green
cascading up.

Cocktail Party, circa 1960

At the party my mother sits at the bar
by the dial phone, smiling for the camera.
In the foreground there are open bottles
of liquor and martini glasses, but my mother
looks sober, smooth-faced and young,
one chiffon shoulder strap sliding down
her soft shoulder. She's wearing her original
nose and large clustered rhinestone earrings.
In the darkened background my father sits
watching her as though she's a fantastic,
wild creature he's afraid might get away.
But why would the hen leave the handsomest
fox in the room? He's honest, a good
provider. She has seen his soft parts.
He hopes she will forgive him.

Genome

What I am made of
came from a star
erupted from Earth
crawled out of the teeming sea
emerged from the swamps
and sands of Africa
arose from the dust of Israel
trooped into Asia
stormed across the steppes
scattered over Europe
climbed onto the rocks of Britannia
spoke every language
of all of those parts
and passed on like a relay baton
the evolving mix of genes
that would become me,
would empower me to pass down
blue eyes and brown
an rh negative gene
the bumpy arm skin that my sister
and our daughters share
the long back
the arched brow
the love of words and song
a stubborn strain of laziness
heart disease, asthma, arthritis
and generations of sons
who will one day
end up bald

Clean Dog

The clean dog is lying
on the tile floor.
His eyebrows wiggle
as I tap the keyboard.
There's the scar on his snout
like a line on a map
where the vet removed
a growth; when he looks
up at me I see the sickle-moon
whites of his eyes.

He is waiting for the next
good thing: his dinner,
a scratch on the rump,
a night-time walk
with the moon peering
through the clouds
which he won't see
for he'll be exploring
with his snout in the bushes:
other dogs, cats, possums,
raccoons, and maybe even
discarded food.

And I'll be thinking,
since the moon will be full
and high, how it looks
like a place
you could climb up to
with the right ladder,
an opening in the sky
to a different world
where the sun always shines
and the beloved are immortal

Dark Matter

I think of the universe expanding,
imagine a big net sack like the kind
old ladies use in Russia that start out
small and grow large to fit

the loaves of bread, cans of fish,
bottles of vodka, juice, and milk—
all the items she can scrounge
on her icy trip home. The universe

expands like the heart expands
to love every child you'll ever have,
to love everything you can love,
even after you're sure you can't possibly
love anything or anyone that much again.

I imagine the universe as a great big sack
growing ever fuller with the souls
of every living thing that has ever existed
in this world.

I think this is where we're headed
when the Earth tires of us
—we too will join the many souls
in the vast sack of the universe, become part

of the dark matter that moves its mystery
upon existence, bending light, spinning
galaxies, sending the souls of the departed
hurtling into our dreams.

Cows

Cows take things as they come.
They are big enough to command respect
but they don't care whether they get it or not.
They care if there's grass to eat.
They feel the sun and the rain.
They love their calves and accept their bulls
for who they are.
They speak in low resonant voices
that rise up from the depths
of their four stomachs.
They have four stomachs!
They know they have a place in this world
and don't worry about what it is.
Not much pisses off a cow.
As she moves over the yellow hillside,
no other animal has the cow's calm majesty.
See her lying in the shade: she knows
she's the queen of something
but she doesn't care if you know it or not.

Sweet Potato

This is the one I chose
from a bin at the farmer's market
between a pond of parsnips
and a crate of beets:
jaundiced skin, protruding hairs,
flesh scratched and scarred
from its travel through the earth,
sallow statue like some armless
creature dragging its lumpy body
over the earth. There's a bend
where it tapers and rises
(I imagine it reaching
into the earth, searching)
and here on my kitchen table
this tail looks like the head
instead and I realize it's all
upside down. I begin to see
a greater world; this root
and all the other things that reach
into the earth searching
for nourishment are like negative
numbers in a world where up is down
and heads are tails. I imagine cooking
this root creature and eating it
and I wonder if I can.

Your Ocean

I will be your ocean
I will follow your eyes
with my horizon
Buoy your gaze on my face
of shining coins
Send my scent to you
over motioning air
and my voice to you
in your dreams

I will lay my great body
before your darkness
Wear your swath of light
like a slick and shining stole
Gather you into the vast reaches of me
where there will be no sense
of fear or shame: I will rise

and bump against your docks
raise your vessels high up
on my tide, carry you sleeping deep
within my murmuring body;
with only the scrape of sand
and shell to wake you
my cool, dark hips will pull you
back to sleep

After Rain

A rainbow arcs
over city and sea
stretching into dark cloud
it speaks to me
in the voice of a harp
playing all the notes from red
to violet, and back again
but it trails off
there's never an ending
to its song, rippling like water
down falls of chartreuse,
vermillion, indigo, gold—
one foot disappearing among
the downtown buildings
the other dissolving
in the storm-brown sea.

Killing the Orchids

People keep giving me orchids.
They're so strange and precious-looking
that I don't know what to do with them.
They're like children that I somehow
can't come to love. They stare at me
with their perfect, imploring faces
and I have to avert my eyes
because I can't answer them. I feel them
watching from their pots on the table.
I can't bring myself to look at them.
Then one day I happen to glance their way
and see that some of those faces
have already crumpled up and browned.
The others will soon follow suit.
All that will be left is a shriveling stem.
I will have done it again.

Blame

Who did this?

Who left the oven on
The door unlocked
The dirty dishes in the sink?

Who left the cat outside
The window open
The bill unpaid?

Who broke the dish
Spilled the milk
Bought the overripe mango?

Who is that fool
Who makes all the mistakes?

Who is that fool
Who thinks it matters?

What's done is done, man.
The earth rolls around.
The moon circles the earth.
The universe expands.

The bulbs someone planted
In October
Push their green fingers

Through the dirt in spring
And no one asks
Who did that?

The Body of God

Form is emptiness, emptiness is form. Heart Sutra

Cold tile beneath bare feet
They say you are made mostly
Of space
Cool mud beneath the blades of grass
You too, and your grass sticking up
Are mostly space
They say that space is everywhere
That we part it with our bodies
Yet still it fills us
That it is why we are humming
With life, that even sitting still
Like this oaken table
We are not merely taking up space
But are infused with it
That no matter what we do
Or think or feel
There is no getting out of this
We are forever filled with this space
And this space is God
So God is all around and in us
And all of us forever dwell
In the body of God.
For some of us
That is all we need to know.

Full of Life

You are so full of life.
When I see you
I'm looking at all of you.
You are a walking colony,
a collection of organisms
on a mobile structure.

When I say I love you
it's not the other creatures—
bacteria and all that—
that I'm talking about
or even your body;
it's You inside your body
that I love

but maybe it is you
and your body
and all those hop-along
organisms that I love

for what is any of this
but a collection
of electrons and nuclei
which must in turn
be made of something
smaller—

It's too much
to think about, but still
it's interesting to note
that even the dead
are full of life.

Big Bang Theory

They say the sound of the Big Bang
must have been more like a deep hum,
an A note too low for a human ear
to detect. I'm disappointed.

I've always imagined it was more
like God slamming a door.
Maybe it was after a fight with his wife
over the fact that she had copied him
and made a world of her own.

I imagine their estrangement
as her world and his continue
along parallel paths, but her beings
cooperate ceaselessly with one other
and the only conflict anyone
ever has to deal with is sex—
the pull of attraction and the resistance,
bodies colliding joyously,
perhaps in defiance of gravity.

God can't get over her nerve
but since the Big Bang,
when he slammed the door
and then punched his fist into the wall
to make Hell, he can't get it up to make
another explosion and now, well,
why bother? He knows that someday
we're gonna do it for him.

Missing Whom

I'm already missing Whom.
Whom has been good to us.
There are times when Who
just won't do; sometimes,
Who is just too abrupt.

Don't get me wrong—I'm not
talking smack about Who.
Who does stuff. Who climbs.
Who builds things. Who falls
in love, has children, tries
to make the world a better place.

Whom is always the receiver
of the love, of the children,
of the betterment of the world.

But when Who is not doing good
or doing neutral, Who also
starts wars, steals, murders,
and rapes. And Whom then
has to be the victim.
It's the way of the world.
If we get rid of Whom,
there won't be anyone to take
the blame, bear the brunt,
or even be the beloved one.

I say, if we remove Whom,
we have to also get rid of Who.
We'll all just have to learn
to stop asking questions.

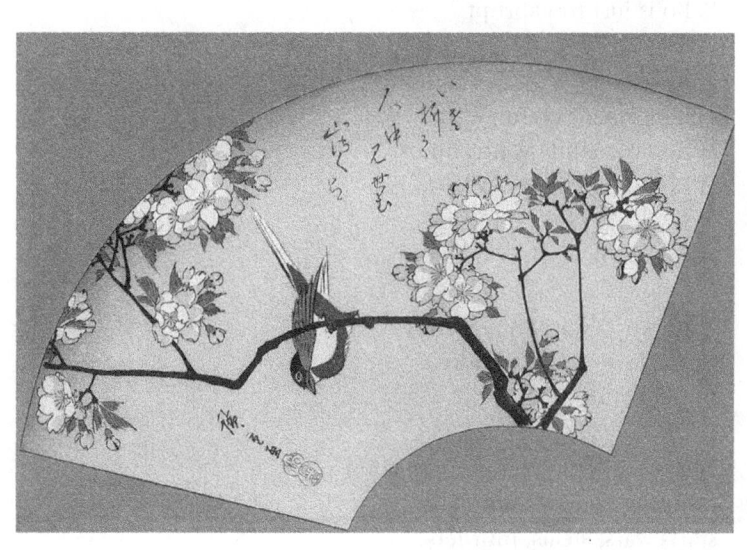

Aida

Catfish McDaris

I Love You

As long as I can
draw a breath or
take a step or open
and close my eyes

As long as my heart
beats or a tear can
travel down my cheeks

Even when I can no
longer see or speak
or write and I am
cold and dead

I will love you

I love you now
forever always

This is the only
important thing
I've ever written

Now forever always
I love you.

Waiting With My Baby

Standing at the bus stop
in a blinding blizzard,
snow blankets the ugly

Cuddling hugging kissing
singing old Beatles songs,
making up forgotten words

The #15 bus is late, but
who cares, I'm with her

Our hearts keep us warm,
we do the bump and shake
our booties catching diamonds
on our tongues, melting them
by touching lips

Let it snow forever
I'm warm all over,
waiting with my baby.

Melt Into Arms

My daughter brought home
a book of God's blessings
drawn by her second grade
class: rainbows, trees, animals,
the sun, I was impressed, but . . .

A friend's four-year-old daughter
was dying of leukemia, she'd
had numerous blood transfusions
and now she had AIDS

The little innocent angel slipped
and fell in the grass and all her
teeth broke off and her hair is gone

And my faith

How do you draw love? Or God?
Or hopelessness?

I want to rip the sun from the sky,
if I could only save this little girl,
but life continues

I wonder if I can or want to,
then my daughter wants me to
hold her and wrap her up safe.

Horses of Elizabeth and Aida

On the azure mountain of
Elizabeth only horses lived,
frolicking in the golden sunlight.

The verdure placid ocean
washed upon its feet.

A comet from the sky turned
the world into a maelstrom,
land became sea and sea, land.

Only the horses lived,
beneath the waves,
seahorses in the magenta
coral reef of Aida.

Dreams That Didn't Work Out

It was Benito Juarez's birthday
when Aida decided we should
move from the north to Puebla

I'd never lived in Mexico, but my
Spanish was past the un poco stage,
we got a nice inexpensive casa

I set up my typer in the bedroom,
the window overlooked a magnificent
waterfall: parrots and monkeys played
in the surrounding jungle flora

Determined to crank out a screenplay
about a woman's hard times picking
cotton and chiles in New Mexico

Hoping Hollywood would make it into
a movie and we could use the money
to buy farmland, for olives and horses

I wanted to build our house by hand
and fish and raise bees for honey, looking
toward the river I watched the beautiful
women with long dark hair doing laundry
on the rocks and I fell asleep.

God's Love

I see God
in my wife's
smile and in
the eyes of
our daughter

I feel God
when I touch
them and know
He is watching
over us and
all things.

Whispers of Painted Women

Drove my Ford down
to Nashville, I couldn't
play guitar very well

All I had was hope and an
old Samsonite full of poems,
I made the rounds of
all the recording studios

Ran out of gas in front
of a house of ill repute,
after hearing out all the
painted women I wrote
down their sad dreams

I listened to their blues then
headed west to the valley of
the chiles hanging crimson

At night I slept under a Li Po
moon while horses danced
and licked my face awake.

Para Siempre

My heart is on
fire when I look
into your eyes

The universe can
never contain
my feelings for you

Many times I've
caused you sorrow
I beg your forgiveness

Without you the world
would be dark, no sunlight
could ever warm me

I love you I love you

My tears run like rivers
my blood turns canyons
into oceans and seas

I am empty without you,
death or life can never
stop my love for you.

Undoing the Done

Fragmented shards of kaleidoscope
mirror reflect our last tango, if I
could only rewind our movie of life

And undo the done, I would throw
ambition and greed out the window

The haunting moon illuminates the
maddening loneliness and slow suicide
tick of a clock in our empty house of
decapitated yesterdays

Invisible laughter reverberates chasing
phantom memories of happiness
into pacing enigmas of desire

Room after room holds no love only
the castrating hate that leaves me
imploding like fireflies into the stars.

My Heart Belongs to You

When I hear
the song
Pretty Woman

I think
of you

How your
brown eyes
sparkle and
your heart
is pure

I could never
love another

My life would
be empty with
out your love

As I grow old
I pray to God
to be taken
first and not
be left alone.

Funeral of a New Mexican Bricklayer

The tiny angelic girl
gave me a purple thistle,
it stabbed my hand, but
the beauty and pain
seemed appropriate

Ladies wept, men
waited for drink,
family fumbled grief

Vultures and ravens
hovered and the worms,
the hungry worms
waited for my father

Antelope watched from
far away as I placed a
Rose brick trowel and a
half empty bottle of Four
Roses whiskey on the
freshly turned ground.

Thanking the Sky

Serrated clouds herringbone
the blue gray sky in speckled
trout belly colored wisps

A nun in coal black and virgin
white smiles with compassion
at the rosy cheeked children

As they escape the edifice of
education, our lady of perpetual
confession and tuition

My little girl's smile when she
sees me makes my heart almost
leap from my proud chest

I grin at the sky, bow my head
and say a silent prayer of thanks.

Lost But Not Crippled

My words are tequila rain
Drowning misery in crudo radiance
Sad people choking on green paper
Thin iguanas swimming in acid rivers
Muted guitar strings singing lonely love
Buried pain clawing anguished hearts
Trees of knowledge raising naked arms
Defiled earth spewing putrid poisons
Polluted oceans spawning blind mermaids
Laughing children ignoring crying grandfathers
Frida's monkey kissing Diego's lips
Gauguin chewing van Gogh's ear
Zapata's moustache inspiring brave warriors
Bulging piñatas dodging giggling muchachos
Pablo having a blue period
Fluttering moths dancing tombstone waltzes

We whisper and shout
Freedom, Love, Peace
But no one stops to listen.

John McDaris

He was supposed to play
sax in the band, nothing
fortified him to be an
infantry platoon leader

Nothing prepared him for
the freezing temperatures
of a Korean winter

He was no hero, no braver
than any other soldier, they
were all afraid, just following
orders from Washington

They marched cautiously
into a quiet village, as night
fell like a guillotine

The only building left standing
was a church, they removed
their helmets & prayed for peace

A whistling sound could be
heard in the silent air, it was
the last they would hear

The high explosive shell killed
them all, it came from an American
ship anchored in a nearby harbor

The medics wrapped what was
left of their bodies & collected
their dog tags for the ones they'd
left back in their own world.

A Broken Heart

Jose met a woman,
he loved so much
he gave her a horse

They disappeared into
the desert together
and were gone three days

When they returned,
they said they were
getting married,
Aida and I were delighted

The night before the wedding,
Jose looked into his woman's
window, she was with
another man

Jose slashed his hand
and smeared blood
all over the window

He jumped on the horse
he'd given her and rode
it to death

Jose didn't speak
for one month, one
morning I got up

He was facing the sun,
tears rolled down his
cheeks, I put my hand
on his shoulder

All he said was,
"Poor horse."

The End of a Journey

I didn't tell Aida or my amigo, Jose
about the news from the doctor,
they sensed something was wrong

Saddling my mustang, I rode to
the top of a mountain that
overlooked everything I loved

God and I had a talk and then I
said adios to the clouds and trees

Tears streamed down Aida's cheeks
as we held each other one last time

Jose painted his face black and
jumped on his horse and galloped
across a meadow screaming my name

I drove through the mountains and
towns and desert without seeing
anything but a blur of wind

The train in Chihuahua took me
through a desert of creosote bushes,
Joshua trees, and mesquite

As we started climbing the Sierra
Madres I watched the canyons drop
off into blue purple black shadows

Closing my eyes I could still see
Aida's face and hear Jose's
scream echoing in my ears
➤

I got a room with a balcony in a
sleepy whitewashed adobe town
at the end of the line

Watching the fishermen bring in
their catch, I waited for the cancer
to finish its feast.

Elizabeth

If I could reach
inside my chest
and rip my heart
out and give it
to you I would

Along with all my
worldly possessions
I would do it gladly

Or turn back the
hands of time and
erase all my faults

If you would forgive
me and speak to me
again after ten long
years of silence

My only child
light of my life
I beg you I need
you I beg you.

IN THE GARDEN

Carolyn Miller

In the Garden

She has it all, Persephone: roots and flowers, dark
and light; her mother, above ground,
baking bread; Pluto, in his shadowy hall,
dressed in black studded with jewels, like a rock star.
In the garden: nosegays of lettuces, cauliflowers like the tight
bouquets of brides; underground, bright carrot torches,
potatoes descending like divers in the darkness,
taproots of cabbages hanging, ghostly stalactites
in the fumey rooms.

Wet earth oozes into her sandals; she parts
fine root hairs, edges past tubers
and rhizomes, past sleeping chipmunks,
curled mice. The only light, faint sun through
gopher holes; the only sound, the animals' slowed breathing.
No days, not even time, just endless corridors
with sow bugs piled along the edges, earthworms
blundering through the walls, and Pluto's loamy chamber,
curtained with webs and lined with fur. All she has to do
is sleep, and love darkness, and surrender
to the night within her.

Until, again, as in a dream, the slumbering ants
and beetles start to stir; above them, soil grows warm
and crumbly as brown sugar. Beans curve their necks
like geese, holding aloft the white shell of the mother
between their simple leaves, and the stout
zucchini start their march across the garden bed.
Already, Demeter is waiting in the early light, cradling
a warm and yeasty loaf.

Cold Spring Suite

Oxalis rioting in the garden;
I remember how van Gogh
loved yellow.

A garden gone to weeds
and me, leaning
against the greenhouse in the sun.

Leaning against the greenhouse
in the sun—how many years
do I have left?

Lichen creeping up the sides
of the deck—
everything just wants to live.

Fleas, bedbugs, mosquitoes—
the Chinese poets
were never really alone.

Magenta of wild sweet peas;
ruby throat of
a hummingbird.

A small hawk overhead.
What am I most frightened of
today?

Even after I die
I will keep on spinning
among the flowers.

Tulips so red
they're almost black—
the heart's blood, pumping.

Community Garden

Why can't you want just this: sun and ocean wind
in the eucalyptus trees, old coastal pines,
a city built on hills?

Why can't you love your life, all of it, even
what you think of as your failures
and mistakes, just because it is your life;
why can't you give up the memory of pain and
your longing for the things you do not have?

Another of those bright, windy days
when I can't decide whether I have been blessed
or abandoned, the sharp edge of the continent
straining against the chill winds off the water,
the hard light of afternoon, and
I am trying to understand acceptance, to embrace
what is; down on my knees in the weeds
and the snail tracks, I turn
the sandy, neglected soil of my garden,
trying to love the imperfect world.

Wild Poppies

California poppies everywhere in the community garden, especially on the hill dedicated to native plants, as if drawn there by the cream cups and the lupine, the wild irises and the one lone mariposa lily. All painstakingly nurtured by garden volunteers, the poppies volunteers as well, like the tiny bumblebees wallowing in pollen. When I wondered how the poppies knew to flock here, Vicki said she believed that flowers could talk. And I thought: Or they might murmur, or they might sing, like whales: *We want to live! We want to live!* Like Marilyn, who told me, toward the end, about the rush of gratitude she felt each morning when she woke to see the light coming through her curtains. Until one morning she did not, and died without ever seeing Italy. Not Rome in summer, people sitting with their feet in the Fountain of the Sinking Boat, alongside the flower seller's roses. Or Venice in the spring, wisteria everywhere, its death-in-life, life-in-death flower falls, its baroque *escaliers*, its aria: *You are here, alive with us; drink deep of this perfume.*

City Garden

Buildings of many sizes and colors
stood along the hard, paved streets.
Flowers opened to the light; fog
poured over the western hills.
People were in machines, words were everywhere, everything
was moving.
    A mess of pigeons with rainbowed necks
scrabbled on their hooked pink feet by the empty
bocce ball courts.
    The tide was in; little peaks
of gray water flung themselves against the shore.
In the water, an elegant loon
with black and white summer wings
dove for fish.
    As I walked up the hill below Black Point,
by the Spanish gun emplacements, abandoned buildings
crumbled on Alcatraz, and wild sweet peas and fennel and
nasturtiums bloomed on the rocky hillside, their colors of orange
and yellow and purple and magenta startling in the fine
gray air.
    Closed, silvery pods of eucalyptus lay in the grass;
in my garden, snails in their armor
hid under the thyme. Grackles and doves and cabbage butterflies
sailed by.
    The soil of the garden was warm
to my touch; oil from the herbs perfumed my skin. A bumblebee
wobbled among the lavender spikes. Under my hands
and feet were infinite worlds. Above me
were infinite worlds in the air and sky.
I breathed in and out. Every leaf was moving
in the ocean wind.

For Nancy

I went to my garden today to dig up the crabgrass;
it's choking the roses and invading the nearby
community plots. I got a shovel out of the tool shed
and cleaned up most of one path and started around the roses,
but the soil is like rock there, thick with sideways crabgrass stems
and the roots they put down from their nodes. Soon I was pouring
with sweat, but I kept on digging, thinking of you and all the things
you loved: linen, beauty, French shoes, silly poems,
terrible puns, orchids, and always, roses. I remembered the deep well
of sorrow inside you for the bitterness of the world, along with your
fine understanding of how so much of life is folly.

I'll never get rid of this crabgrass; it keeps growing under the ground
where you can't see it except when it slants up out of the dirt, green
and jagged. Still, my roses are thriving: Cécile Brunner,
Blanc Double de Colbert, the fragile Heritage you gave me. I thought
   about how,
of all the months, you died in May, when roses were blooming
   everywhere:
Abraham Darby, flushed with pink and peach and coral; Fair Bianca,
with her scent of musk; Fragrant Cloud, to carry you on your way.

Blake's Garden

William saw angels in the trees, large ones,
writing in their books, their wings almost scraping
on the ground, their lustrous hair falling in their eyes
as they traced glowing letters on the page, taking notes
on greengages and vegetable marrows and aubergines,
surrounded by a strange perfume like lilies
mixed with pepper and the faintest whiff of sandalwood,
encircled by auras of sacred fire like fog burning off water,
as the sun beamed down on William Blake and his small
    garden,
where snails slept under the nasturtiums
and foxgloves stood like flaming swords
lighted by God's hand.

Susan's Garden

I sat down by the nasturtiums
hard by the compost heap.
The summer grass was already brown
and high fog was billowing in,
great cloud-animals passing over me in herds.
Bees followed their jagged routes among
the open flower mouths, and far off
I could hear the high-pitched, sustained calls
of foghorns. I lay down in dry grass, sun
touching me all over, thinking
thank you, thank you, thank you.

Rose Garden, Summer Solstice

Everyone here believes that the roses
are blooming only for them, here where the air
by the formal beds is layered with the scent
of roses. From deep in their flushed and darkening hearts
pour odors of lemons and pepper, apricots, honey,
vanilla and myrrh and musk and semen, apples and quince,
raspberries and wine and ocean, the faint
scent of blood and the fragrance of death and the breath
of the life we are living now, in this place
where the roses are blooming for each of us, alone.

Another Summer Solstice

Sound of foghorns streaming out
above the backyard

ripening tayberries, spindly pear tree
hung with tiny pears

pollen falling down the throats
of foxgloves

someone speaking Spanish,
laughter in another garden

nothing to fear this day in June
sun pouring down

leaf shadows trembling on
the old green linen tablecloth

poets writing in their journals how
not even time can touch them here

November 10

So the day ends, dragging its perfumes with it. The crows settle down in the fractured Monterey pine. The sun hovers, pulsing, on the horizon, spreading its coppery light over everything. The entire dying garden holds its breath. Goodbye, goodbye, my sad, tired, thrilling, redeeming day.

Garden in Late Winter

Lost fragrance lost blossoms some cold green
eruptions jar lids and netting a few small
violas old upturned buckets and glass jars and wood chips
seed heads and snail trails leggy arugula dead vines
of green beans rotted nasturtiums rosemary blaring its little blue
bugles chamomile sprouting and lettuces bolting
small brown birds searching nigella seeds bursting
their paper pods dead heads of sunflowers blackened
and flattened everywhere yellow-white fibers of
exploded artichokes still on the stem armored
like dragons sending their seed clusters out to the
wet dirt exposed roots and tubers oxalis springing
litter fermenting neglected and wizened weak
sunlight spilling over the Swiss chard and scaffolding
tilted my heart slowly opening like a dark bulb

Where the Stars at Night Are Big & Bright

Joan Jobe Smith

Deep in the Heart of Texas

Other than the winter when I was born in
Paris, Texas, I've only been to Texas twice
and on the way, right in the middle of Texas
near Denton or Sweetwater, someplace in
the middle of the night and nowhere where
there's not one tree or hill, one, just flat land
falling off the thousand corners of the Texas
earth, my father parked the car on the side of
the road and he, my mother, and me, got out
of the car to look at the stars, the sky a big
round black dome filled with so many sugar
crystalline stars that the sky dripped white as
vanilla cake icing and my father stood in
front of the car lights as if on a stage and sang
that song which should be Texas's state song
as loud as he could into the big, round-bright
night: "The stars at night are big and bright—"
and then he clapped his hand five times and
went on singing Deep in the Heart of Texas . . .

Green When It Rained

When it rained was when my mother sang
her sweetest as she cooked supper in the
kitchen. "Ohh," she'd whisper, fogging up
the window with her breath. "Look at the
beautiful rain, how green the world, the
leaves, when it rains. Rain now means
food to eat next year. Do you understand?"
No, I didn't. We lived in southern California
in the 1950s in the eternal plentitude midst of
supermarkets, farmers markets selling food
grown in nearly cornfields and orange groves.
Dairies with fat cows surrounded us, jingling
ice cream men and bakery trucks filled with
sweets and hot bread drove up and down
our streets. In between her songs, Amapola,
my pretty little poppy, you'll never know
how much I love you, always, she'd tell me
of yellow Texas droughts and brown famine
how she searched shadow gullies for greens
when she was a little girl, stole corn, peaches
and pecans from rich folks' fields and orchards.
I'd never gone hungry nor had to steal or search
for my food and her sweet soprano tales of
hunger filled me with so much wanting that come
suppertime as I mashed the buttery, Texas-style
potatoes, I scraped spotless the pot with the spoon
to lick every speck. grateful to all the gods
of cornucopia, ambrosia, and green Mother Rain.

Texas Girl as Dainty as a Lady From Kent

To get a good job in California during World War 2
my Texas mother went to the British movies
to lose her Texas accent, affect an English
tone and, a good mimic, able to imitate
Mrs. Miniver or Wendy Hiller's Eliza
Doolittle talking Cockney, my mother
passed for a native Californian, got jobs
at nice cafes with signs in the window: "NO
Okies or Texans need apply!" and for a while
told a sad story to get that good job at a fine
hotel in San Francisco that she was a British
War Bride married to a Scotsman (which my
father really was, though born in Texas, too,
and a Medic in the U.S. Army). People must
often tell tall tales about their origins others
find awful, but none of them ever enjoyed
the charade as much as my mother, a natural
actress who would fluff her chocolate-colored
hair, practice her "ahhs" and "ohhs" and "thahnk
yew veddy muches" until her Texas twang elided
sky-toned glottal birdsong, her malaprops and
dangling modifiers charming onomatopoeia
Americana as she learned to sip her coffee,
icy Coca Colas, and eat her fat hamburgers
with pickle and tomahtoes with a pinky finger a-flit
as snootily, as daintily as a Lady from Kent.

Peach Tree Santa Claus

Armed with a double-barrel shotgun, my
young grandmother Nora Ely was told by
her daddy to go shoot the ears off that
no-good poacher stealing peaches out in
their orchard outside Paris, Texas, in 1910,
when it was okay to shoot poachers, cattle
rustlers and barn burners and when my
Grandma Nora found the poacher up in the
top of a peach tree, chomping on a peach,
peaches stuffed in his shirt fat as a Peach Tree
Santa Claus, my Grandma Nora aimed her
shotgun between his eyes and she was a good
shot, good with a horsewhip, too, could swat
flies so fast she sliced them in half and I saw her
do it when she was 62 and when the poacher
saw her, a pretty little woman wearing a yellow
satin ribbon in her hair, he smiled, a handsome
devil, a cowboy with black curly hair and on
the spot, that shotgun pointed at him, asked her
to marry him and she did and they had 7 kids,
one my beautiful, black curly-haired mother.
They write tons of Peach Tree Santa Claus love
songs about falling in love with a stranger across
a crowded room on a slow boat to China or beneath
a blue moon, even the Beatles saw you standing there
on a magical mystery tour and wanted to hold your
hand in strawberry fields forever and the first
thing I did when I bought my house with that
big Texas-size backyard was plant a peach tree.

Born Not to Laugh at Tornadoes

It was the only time I ever saw my father
afraid, someplace in the middle of Texas,
on our way in 1948 from California to
Dallas, a tornado out there, stick-still
on the edge of the world, black-circled
by a steel-cloudy sky, a tornado like an
exclamation mark in a small book so far
away but yet right behind my father's
left ear as he drove his black jackrabbit
LaSalle running for its life 100 miles
per hour, no storm cellars in those parts,
not even a gas station, just dirt all around
and telephone poles toothpick horizon time
and that tornado curlicueing now like a
question mark and doing a little hula
next to my father's brow, my father chain-
smoking, grinding his teeth, my mother not
speaking, just twisting the radio knobs
for tornado news or music or anything besides
static to drown out the wind outside blowing
Texas up our fenders. Were they coming at you
when they stood still or when they moved like
that? they asked each other but neither knew,
they'd been little kids asleep in bed back then
in Texas when tornadoes hit towns nearby
and my father got that La Salle to do 125
on Route 66 for half an hour and finally
the tornado was way behind us, a mere comma
and it began to pour down rain, lightning
and thunder all around and in Denton the sun
came out and Hank Williams came on on the radio
and my father laughed and said,
"Christ, if that don't beat all."

Sweethearts of the Purple Sage Beneath the Starry Skies Above

My father always said that my
mother was so pretty because she
was a Texas Girl and Texas had the
prettiest women in the whole world
and this would please my mother so
and make her smile she would let him
embrace her in front of me, she'd
sit on his lap, no mention of
that when a Texas Girl she'd
picked cotton, worn flour-sack dresses
and couldn't go to school winters
because she had no shoes, the bad
and sad things never mattering,
when you wear moon-glow gardenias
in your dark chocolate-colored hair
black suede high heels on your feet
the old hard times easy as Eden
once you're all grown up and pretty
and sitting on a happy man's knee.

More Secrets About Beans

Beans meant a lot to me
when a kid disliking meat,
beans the favorite meal
my mother fixed, but my
father who'd grown up in
Texas Dust Bowl poverty
of the 1930s where a pot of beans
meant eking out a living
as well as Sunday supper
loved meat, big T-bones, thick
roasts, pork chops. Meat
on his plate meaning not just
luxury, deliciousness and
plentitude, but also, so he
thought, good health, so my
mother's once-a-week pot of
pintos and corn bread because
she craved them was always a
meatless bone of contention
between them. Beans still
mean a lot to me, a big pot
of them my favorite soup to
cook, especially on a cold
winter day when I'm all alone
and the steam fogs up the
windows, encasing me, making me
feel special and wrapped up
as if I were a good-news secret
and I like how the bubbling
warmth actually speaks to me
and I understand
every word.

Gene Autry Rides Again

Sneaking me sips of his black rot-gut coffee
when I was 3, my grandpa Old Robert showed me
how to roll my own cigarette with one hand from
a pouch of tobacco he closed with this false teeth
and while he smoked the twisted thing I'd lit
with a wooden matchstick learning to play with
fire safely, he told me Gene Autry before ol' Gene
got rich and famous was a pal of his back in Texas
in the 'teens when they were cowpokes on the
Chisum Trail. Over the Red River ol' Gene and him'd
go driving those l'il' dogies up through Oklahoma
and Missouri where my grandpa taught ol' Gene to
hogtie and lasso and shoot straight with this gun my
grandpa still had in his holster in 1943 modern-day
San Francisco, a real old pistol and Old Robert could
still shoot straight as he did at 22 and proved it the
next week when my father came around to woo back
my mother who was mad at him, told him to go away
and when he wouldn't my grandpa shot into the air
just two inches from my father's right ear that left a
ringing in his ear for the next 5 years. And decades
later after Old Robert died I found out his Gene Autry
tales were true, plus more: he'd taught young Gene
everything Gene knew and at a Texas rodeo in 1933
Gene yelled over a microphone for Old Robert to stand
up and take a bow and everyone hooted and clapped
and later Gene gave my grandpa $100 and a big pat
on the back and all grown up I learned to shoot a gun,
too, beer cans and bottles between the eyes, but I never
smoked nor drank rot-gut coffee and later when I was
a go-go girl I danced some of the Texas steps my grandpa
taught me and doing a jig to the Beatles' Ob-la-di-ob-la-da
one night at the Whisky a Go Go as I imagined a rodeo
of bucking broncos and Stetson hats the most fun I ever had.

The Red River

A navigable river in south central United States, 1,018 miles long, it rises in the high plains in east New Mexico, flows east crossing the Texas Panhandle and then becomes a boundary between Texas and Arkansas, turns south in southwest Arkansas and crosses the border into Louisiana, flows southeast across Louisiana into the Mississippi River into the Gulf of Mexico and I was born in Paris, Texas, 30 some miles from the Red River and first time I saw it in 1953 it was brown muddy as old chocolate when we drove over it in my father's new Ford Fairlane on Christmas Day to see my grandpa Old Robert dying of TB in an Oklahoma hospital, my grandma Nora weeping in the back seat beside me. I had to wait in the cold car with the dog, little kids made old folks sick they said and on the way back to Paris crossing over the Red River again my grandma Nora told us about the big flood of 1914 when a big old 100-year-old pecan tree like that big one over there fell over into the river. Folks came for miles to save it, an Eiffel Tower, its roots Goliath arms reaching for the sky. Hundreds of folks pulled and pushed and tugged and heaved ropes tied to the tree trunk and branches while the Red River raged wild and turned maroon and almost drowned a lot of them. For days the folks camped out, stubborn as only Texas and Oklahoma homesteaders can be and they saved it just fine and come spring of 1915 the pecan tree rewarded the folks with the biggest bumper crop ever known, horns of plenty of plenty of pecans, three thousand pecan pies it must've made, all the women doubling up pecans in each pie, four cups instead of two, to float on top the brown sugar custard, not one pecan orphan losing its way from that tree, not one pecan gone afloat, uneaten Ishmael down below in that dirty old Gulf of Mexico.

The French're Much Different from Me and You

Uncle Ray on Christmas Day did not call
from Hot Springs, Arkansas, the way he
has for the past ten years to say: Howdy
Niece, How're y'all? so I could say, Uncle
Ray, I went to Paris last summer! *France*,
Uncle Ray, not Paris, Texas, where I was
born in 1940 and Uncle Ray in 1923. Paris,
France, where he, a G.I. Joe in 1945 marched
down the Champs-Élysées with his troops on
his way to the Arc de Triomphe to receive a
Croix de guerre from General Charles de Gaulle
for bravery for escaping twice from Nazi POW
camps and saving his men from machine guns.
Wanted to tell Uncle Ray I'd thought of him as
I strolled that same path, 2012, perhaps my
red sandals stepping in the same spot as Uncle
Ray's brown, worn-down 1945 Army boots.
I was brave, too, dodging traffic, motorcycles,
bicycles, taxis, limos, Rolls-Royces, to stand
in the middle of the Champs-Élysées to take
a photo of the Arc de Triomphe to send him.
Uncle Ray would've laughed at that and for
sure told me again how General de Gaulle
after he pinned the Croix de guerre on my
Uncle Ray's chest, kissed both of his cheeks.
"General de Gaulle didn't mean nothin' by it,
honey," Uncle Ray might've said again. "Men
kissing men like that's just the way the French do.
The French're much different from me and you."

Uncle Ray on New Year's Day Long Distance
from Hot Springs, Arkansas, Calls to Say

He's just had his 3rd Pacemaker installed. They
(the HMOs) make you wait now till the old ones
break down so he couldn't move for 6 whole days;
couldn't take no anesthesia while they did the new
one, he's almost 85, too old, so they did a local but
he's okay and I say, Oh, goodness (hating HMOs).
But he can take it, I know: Uncle Ray's had a metal
plate in his head since age 18 when he escaped twice
in World War 2 from 2 German POW camps and he
goes on to say my cousin Charles Douglas Smith
down in Austin got hit and got run down by a drunk
woman driver on his motorcycle (Uncle Ray's two-
step Texas syntax, not mine) and after two surgeries
Doug's okay and Uncle Ray says he read that poem
of mine I sent him about the Red River. Did I know
they once lived right by it in Texas and Yes, I say
and one time his Daddy the cowboy, my granddaddy,
herded cattle across the Red River when it was a mile
wide and I imagine a mile-wide Red River, raging
bittersweet chocolate and wonder: How's it possible
to cross a mile-wide river without a bridge? Wonder
how's it possible to escape twice from 2 POW camps
with shrapnel in your head? Stay alive through open
heart surgery without anesthesia? Motorcycle miracle,
Pacemaker catastrophe and Uncle Ray says did you
hear about all them blackbirds that dropped dead out
of the sky yesterday here in Arkansas? Yes, I say and
he says how he and my Aunt Ernestine will be married
65 years come June and they don't send Christmas cards
no more because Ernie can't hold a pen to write no more
and Uncle Ray don't know how to spell—ha-ha-ha-he
laughs—because he only went to 3rd grade. But you're a
hero, escaped twice when you were only 18 from German
POW camps during World War 2, shrapnel in your head,
I say, and Uncle Ray laughs again and says, Aw, honey,
if it'd happened to you, you'd'a done the same thing.

Letting Go of Ashes

Rick Smith

The Need for Miracles
   (for Val Sigstedt, stained glass maker)

When we become uncomfortable in our weeping
we scan for miracles on bark,
for evidence glistening
on our fingertips.
Stigmata for the seekers,
postcards from the holy trinity.

They slide Erika into the MRI chamber
on rails. She is counting crickets.
She loves the sound of crickets.
The ceiling of the lab is sky blue
so she sees it just before the disordered percussion of
jackhammer and submarine sound
takes over. She sees an eggshell grid
and can almost touch it with her tongue. It's
best not to look but if she can see
sky or grass before she slides in,
it helps. Healing is blue and it is green.
Stained glass shards and panels in
lead grooves up high. Rose, green, sky blue
shards hold her place in sanity.
In fact, if one piece is missing, she will notice.

Some red
in that canopy
could save a life too.
Fireflies in June, sunrise over the Delaware.
Or where we live now,
by the groves,
the smell of them:
blood oranges & fever rising.

This time a handful
of broken glass
delivers us from the need
for other miracles.

North Light
    (for Mama Smith)

Upstairs,
the smell of turpentine
and cadmium red,
oil rags and gesso pads.
It's what we've always known.

And downstairs, you're cooking
mussels and artichokes,
steam rising from pots.
And the radio is always
between stations.

There is north light
and sometimes flame,
a brain pan in heat.
It's a signature,
like Imelda's blue espadrilles,
Batista's jeep,
like the toothy whistle
of "Sweet Georgia Brown",
it makes things snap and tick.

At 75 and
stark naked,
holding yourself up
with a cane:
a self portrait in pencil
and the point
is not
how good you look.

You could live in Chinatown,
join your neighbors for tai-chi at dawn
under the Williamsburg Bridge.
➤

After,
you could walk it off,
the chill of the East River,
steam
off the perfect teacup.
The thing you could not teach me
I am able to learn on my own.

Here,
you're wearing a straw hat,
no shoes,
and you hold a paint brush
like a baton, no,
a weapon,
landscape in flight:
the sun, the lilies, the river.
A small canvas is taut and
returns the favor.
It fights you,
has a will of its own
just the way you like it.

The button of a heart
I can feel
even at my wrist
and throat.
The pump and pull
of life in my palm,
the way I hold you,
its all true

Re-Entry
(for sister Kim)

July bakes the street.
We have to wait
until 4 a.m.
for this heat
to dissolve into dawn
so sleep can come.

You appeared
above the island
where bad water defines boundaries,
where hard lines
are everywhere.

I waited for you
in the street,
looking up
at the hospital window.
You were squirming,
pale and restless
under a perfect blanket
left by a well wisher.
And the street burned.

It's 1951.
Stevenson is fading in the polls.
The Dodgers,
taken from behind,
collapse in the stretch.
There is big trouble
on the 38th parallel
but someone comes flying
out of smoke and rubble
in a stolen MIG-15.
➢

It's you in the cockpit,
fumbling with landing gear.
A 3-point landing
over bad water,
a narrow runway,
rubber squealing.
You,
slipping
through a seam
in the sky.

Mad Woman Bending Light
    (after the photographer, Christina Fernandez)

I picture you holding a Leica,
snapping the shutter
and there is bowed light.
You are balanced on the last narrow step
above some tomb in Mexico,
bending that light all by yourself,
putting a little english on God's curve.

And who is holding you up
while you lean into that
darkest space,
coaxing light,
teetering on the thinnest,
the narro-
west of
steps?
There are arched gates, they
open away from you,
tempt you off-balance
like a dark valentine
and now the light is at the back of you:
a Spanish girl
bending light like a mad woman,
teetering on the edge with
eyes wide
seeing it all without blinking.
I picture you never blinking
at all.

hands that hold
    (for Jean Valentine)

again the chaos
kettle drum prestissimo
blows my chest apart

against a wall
that yields
to the pounding

and becomes something
more than the eye or ear
can manage

submerges me
in the sweet foam
of an ancient river

if i can breathe
and rise to another surface,
a surface of light

where notes blend
and hang on rhythm,
i could find myself

crossing a white bridge
to hands that hold me,
lead me:

a path that can only
be seen in
the dark

Saunder at Bedtime

I am in the counting house
until my boy takes my hand,
draws me away from the mathematics
of dread.

Wings of the barn owl move
into a small wind.

First,
he makes a church of my hands
and people come out
to picnic and stretch
in sunshine.

He throws handscapes:
there are paper fish
on strings,
anything that can slip
through fingers.

Jaws snap,
a glowing eye
moves across the ceiling.

Attacked by triangles,
hands return shaking.
The jaw chews at anything
that has shape.
These battles take place above us,
in the safety of stucco.

We watch as
movements of the living
fly around corners
up high
➢

and beyond the impact
of old walls slamming together
and if we giggle
and tumble back in a tangle of limbs,
all the numbers finally work.
Looking up,
we are in conference,
silent as stars.

Saunder on a Swing

I hold your little ankles,
take 2 steps back
while you squeal, "hold me hold me"
and I hold you there
suspended. Your eyes couldn't
get much bigger and when I
let go you throw
yourself into a perfect
backwards arc. Your
amazed face at the top
of the arc
floats: paper
moon on a
Chinese kite,
catching updrafts, sitting
on open space. Then
you fly feet first
back to my steady hands.
You are four and learning to pump,
trusting your trajectory,
learning altitude, riding
high above Beryl Park.
There is no winding down,
there is only defiant, ferocious
and otherwise unqualified
joy in this
brilliant season

Junipers

My son
he puts a night clerk's bell
in front of me and leans on it.
It's all about Italian Junipers
kicking up concrete.

Sometimes he tells me he hates me,
that when he grows up,
he will never come to visit.
Then,
he asks me to watch a video.
He's getting good at the games.
They're all about killing
and blowing up something.

Overturned dump trucks,
brigades of infantrymen
are scattered lifeless
in the yard.

He is fascinated by the junipers
and how they kick up the driveway
in slow motion,
but they kick it up
just the same.

At night when the house is quiet,
I go to his room and whisper
promises into a sleeping ear.

By Love Joined

This is for you
mouth to mouth love.
Eating ham & cream cheese
and reading to me
in bed after a hot bath.

And then we make love
on a windy night
deep under the covers.
And you,
nine thousand miles away
in Athens, thinking of me
and eating ham and cream cheese
on perfectly round crackers.

Early Days

You were screaming at me
outside that café in the rain.
I had just told you what I thought,
that if we stayed together
I'd be doing all day
at fucking San Quentin.
You didn't like what I said,
but you knew it was true.

Anyway, you're quite safe now,
to grow old with a new life.
When I look back,
we both lucked out.
We knew love and death
were dancers
on the same floor,
to have and to hold,
in sickness and in health . . .

Splendor In The Grass, though,
that was the real turnaround.
Then we held hands
through Times Square,
made it all the way
back to the Biltmore
where you finally let me in.
The movie spooked you though.
So I wasn't all the way in.
Till later.
Another night.
And the rooms
were always in your name.
➤

Sometimes, early in love,
we promise more than we possess.
How many letters written,
then torn to shreds?
You can say
time and space will end
but you cannot say
our time on W. 69th St., N.Y.C
will ever end.

So even now,
I write a poem and you appear.
You may never see this one,
but I still say
it was a good time.
And it made the gods smile,
yours and mine,
for a minute.

Erika

   I
A sudden stirring,
the restless, crazy L-shaped scar
carved by window pane
deep into your right arm and
where they sewed you back together,
I run lips
up and down that ragged trail.

   II
Then, in winter,
I'm driving over frozen gravel;
the branches of the cottonwood
are nearly mad with wind
and bending.

   III
The satin slip
drops like snowfall,
noiseless but not truly silent.

There's always a soft hiss to it
in the landing
and then we can't stop laughing.

   IV
The meeting of breath,
hands and feet;
at the crossroads,
I make a wish,
run lips
up that wounded trail.

sequence in a lobby

I watch you
sitting by the palms
in an expensive hotel.
A pair of tiny golden matadors
swing by the throat
at your extra-
ordinary lobes.
They hang there
trembling in space
as you shift
to watch your waiter
disappear through doorways.
You sip at something pink
& when
I approach carrying orchids,
you pretend not to see me.

There is a mural behind the bar,
a gathering of storm clouds
over the desert floor.
You become a woman
in a hurry.
You will not be distracted
by the fact that we are
in the same place
at the same time.
As soon as the road
puts its mouth on you
you will lunge into the future.

I watch you drive away
I am holding orchids
holding on
to nothing
but orchids.

note to the first arrondissement

I'm in the kitchen
at the yellow table
drinking to your new life
and to mine
the sun pushes
a square of light
onto my lap.

eating light

We take breakfast on the lawn:
raw tuna, rice, and beer.
The sun is warmer than usual.
You sit cross legged in the heat.
I am looking up your kimono.
The light is right.

Untitled for Dave

In New York, people seem so busy but everybody there knows this: You dent a parked car, an unattended car, you stop, you leave your name and number on the windshield. So when I back hard into a brand new Capri with my battered Dodge Colt (red, but with one green door that doesn't close all the way), the one with no spare, no radio, the one that's nearly paid off, the one with a glove box full of tickets, a flashlight that sometimes works and road maps of places like the Province of Saskatchewan, I find a pad of notepaper I took from the Wilshire Motel in Oklahoma City (where they do not serve beer) and a crusty blue ballpoint pen bearing the word, "Paxil." A black man with a yellow cane stops to watch. People with not much to do begin to appear on stoops. One is in a racing wheelchair, wheels locked in place. He's poised in mid-hand at a card table set up on the sidewalk. I can tell he likes what he's holding. In the air is a mesmerizing kick drum sampled against a bass line that visits the bones. The group grows restless. I'll bet they are wondering if I'll handle my obligation. I don't know why but I sense some of them are armed. And all of them know the owner of the Capri. Back before there was Valium, there were Saints. I need Our Lady of Perpetual Responsibility to appear by my side, to whisper wisdom and rhyme. The street is straight and narrow, not an angle I can really play. The air goes still, stale smoke sits for a second, waiting for a breeze. I take the blue pen and scribble, "Dear Sir or Madam, people are watching to see if I leave my number. And they're pretty sure that's what I'm doing. Sorry about your car". And I sign it, "Dave". Then I slip the folded white paper under a brand new wiper blade. No one steps forward, no one says a word. I rejoin my Colt, dab at my moist forehead, try to breathe and drive very slowly from the scene, toward West Fourth Street and Sixth Avenue (where they do serve beer). You can feel it, the peace, the serenity; everyone I see has a sense of well being while a cool quarter moon dances on the dark and surly Hudson.

Mural of a lake*

The facts aren't straight,
never have been.
We can see linoleum,
a gum wrapper;
the 2-way AC outlet
gazes back with its screwy eyes
from a nest in the long grass
by the water's edge.
A birch reaches past the paper seams
leaning crazily around
a corner before
drifting off
into ordinary sky.
And then
there's the house.
We rarely speak of the house.
The people in there
keep mostly to themselves
rooted in the knowledge
that nothing is about
to happen.

*From a photograph by Diane Arbus entitled, "A lobby in a building, N.Y.C." (1966).

Letting Go of Ashes

Katy, we
release you into a wind,
into the sand,
scatter you in watery passage
where you recognize
the forms of flight and floating,
of movement without effort,
in a rhythm
that always lived in you.

You lived hard,
like you couldn't be touched.
But you felt something blow
through you
and now definition is around you.
Around you,
the clarity of light,
around you, what remains,
around you, all that you love.
We held you long in life,
then in a canister
inside an old doll house.
We were waiting
for you to stop moving.
It didn't happen.

And here, now,
the wildest Charleston
of them all.

Wasn't Columbus a Bachelor?

Fred Voss

A Genius for Eating

"It's so great that you love my cooking so much!" Jane says
to Frank as she serves him dinner in bed
"No one else ever loved my cooking before
I get to cook my food for you
and you love to eat it!"
Frank sits up in bed watching his favorite movie *Vertigo*
as Jane hands him the tray with the dinner she's cooked for him on it
big golden brown
turkey leg in wonderful-smelling golden gravy with homemade
    delicious stuffing
and steamed broccoli and a big piece of Jane's homemade pumpkin pie
    beside it
and as he bites into the juicy delicious turkey leg Frank thinks
how great it is
in order to make Jane deliriously happy all he needs
is a tongue
and taste buds and salivary glands and throat and intestines moving
in peristaltic motion swallowing and a stomach to receive and digest
his other skills took decades of hard work
to perfect
micrometers and C-clamps and overhead cranes
and machine handles and a 1,600-page Machinery's Handbook
full of speeds and feeds and thread pitch diameters and tap drill
    diameter calculations
and trigonometry and metallurgy and 100-pound vises
he had to lift and crazy foremen
he had to let scream in his face
and images
and metaphors and syntax and rhythms he had to devise
or wait to receive from the muse as he gradually
carved out over the years his own territory and style
as the world's first machinist poet
surviving
firings and long-term unemployment and machinists threatening
    to meet him
in the parking lot with knives and rejections
by poetry magazine editors that made him feel like he should never
    have lifted
      ➤

a pen
now all Frank has to do is say,
"This turkey is the best I've ever tasted in my life!"
and mean it
and Frank works out a little running his tongue around the inside of
    his mouth
as he perfects licking gravy off his teeth and smiles
After shoving hundreds of tons of steel bars into the roaring white-hot
    flames of blast furnaces
it's nice to have a skill that only requires sliding
a turkey leg
into his mouth.

Frank Almost Writes His First Poem About Paris

"Please, Frank,
nearly every poem you write has a concrete floor in it," Jane says
after Frank reads her his new poem about a machine shop with a
    concrete floor in it.
"You've got to write about something else, Frank, something not so
    arduous.
Write about our trip last summer to Paris.
We saw the Eiffel Tower and original van Goghs and Cezannes and
    Notre Dame
and boated down the Seine and saw a surrealistic statue of Rimbaud
James Joyce's original manuscript of Ulysses at Shakespeare and
    Company
and visited Jim Morrison's grave.
Why don't you write about Paris? Something romantic."
"But that's such a cliché!
Everyone who goes to Paris sees Notre Dame and the Louvre and
    Eiffel Tower
and takes boat rides down the Seine and sees Morrison's grave
and writes about it.
If readers want romance they can read *Madame Bovary*. Let them read
    Les Misérables
No one's ever written about greasy shop rags or piles of metal chips
on a concrete machine shop floor the way I have!
Did Flaubert or Hugo or Baudelaire write about a machinist spitting a
    sunflower seed
over the top of an engine lathe or riveting a 'World Class Asshole'
    plaque
to the inside of his toolbox lid?"
Frank takes a big chug from his bottle of beer and sticks out his chest
like Ernest Hemingway.
"Writers should write what they know! What they live!
Not clichés of boating down the Seine, ogling art and an Eiffel Tower!"
Frank smiles a self-satisfied smile
until he sees Jane
glaring up at him from her chair like she always does
when it's obvious he's full of crap
and Frank sips more beer and remembers
their sunset walk alongside the Seine
their fondant au chocolate and champagne at the sidewalk café

➢

in sight of the Eiffel Tower
the Paris July 8 full moon on his birthday shining into the skylight
of their bedroom in their autrement on Rue Beautrellis.
After all, Frank does have to admit
that it is just possible, that for just one poem anyway
to write about lamp-lit, rain-streaked cobblestone streets and
the way the summer sun sparkling between Notre Dame's steeples
turned Jane's auburn hair to a golden flame
could be just a bit more interesting, possibly even more romantic than
a sunflower seed spit over the top of an engine lathe onto a concrete
    floor
and a "World Class Asshole" plaque.

Absent-Minded Poet Laureate Garbage Man

Jane hands Frank a plastic bag full of garbage from the kitchen sink
and asks him to throw it
into the dumpster in the alley and get
her red sun hat in their car in their garage while he's down there
and Frank carries the garbage down and throws it out
but while he is doing it works
on a new poem in his head and forgets
her red sun hat
like he forgot
to tape Jane's favorite Bette Davis movie
not throw
her prized 1980 James Dean T-shirt into the drier
where it shriveled
fill
the gas tank of her car clean
the kitchen sinks with Comet cleanser recharge
the cell phone write
Jane's aunt thanking her for the jar of jaw-breaking hard candy she sent them
all in the last week
because he was working on poems in his head
and Frank smiles
empty-handed when he returns from the alley without her red sun hat
   and says,
"Well, you know they say Einstein always had so much going on in his
   mind
he always had 15 suits all identically the same
in his closet so he would never forget
to put on the right one in the morning,"
Then Frank hangs
his head in modesty and adds,
"Of course, I'm not saying I'm just as smart
as Einstein."
"No, you're just as stupid!" Jane says.

When it comes to a good excuse for a bad memory it appears
Frank's poems are no match
for relativity.

Gallinaceous Xerophyte

During one of Frank and Jane's weekly Sunday morning teatimes in bed
Jane is talking about her days working the go-go bars in the 70s
and how the drunks would think she was a bimbo
just because she danced in a fringed bikini
"I called them gallinaceous xerophytes," she says
sipping her tea
"What!?" Frank says
"If a drunk harassed me and treated me like a bimbo I'd call him
a gallinaceous xerophyte," Jane says
"What's that?"
"Gallinaceous means a bird that picks its food off the ground like a pigeon
eating seeds or pebbles in the alley
Xerophyte means thick-skinned like a cactus or an armadillo or a rhinoceros
I'd call the drunk a gallinaceous xerophyte
just to make fun of him without him knowing it"
Frank tries
to get his head around this and laugh but is reverting to his UCLA graduate school
in English literature days and can't help trying to put the 2 words together in a way
that makes literal dictionary definition sense to him
so he can communicate with Jane on some kind of rational level
"A thick-skinned pigeon?" Frank asks
"A thick-skinned rooster!" Jane says and laughs
"A rooster with skin like a rhinoceros?
How can a rooster have skin like a rhinoceros?
Or an armadillo, how can a pigeon have skin like an armadillo?
What do you mean by that?"
"It's supposed to be funny! Ludicrous! Absurd! You like Ionesco.
How can a rhinoceros be a Nazi?"
Frank slams down his teacup
"But that doesn't make any sense!
Don't you know that those adjectives don't work together!?
What goes on in that brain of yours sometimes?
Who ever heard of a rhinoceros that pecks its food off the ground?!"

➤

255

When Jane sets down her teacup and laughs hysterically
in Frank's face
Frank is about to fly into a rage until he stops
and realizes how clever she is
and how he's treating her like a bimbo
as he looks across their bedroom into the mirror at himself
and sees his very first
gallinaceous xerophyte.

How Sexy Is It To Be Wrong

Driving to work for half an hour Frank is alone
alone
like he was as a bachelor
and though Frank loves his wife Jane very much he can't help thinking
about when he was a bachelor and never had to tell his opinions
to Jane and hear her arguments
about why he was wrong
driving in his car by himself Frank knows
Jim Morrison did *not* pull out his dick on that stage in Miami
van Gogh was not bipolar
Marlon Brando was not an asshole
a man with handwriting that presses through the page (like Frank's)
is not a psychopath
and Frank breathes the dawn air and smiles and looks down cross
    streets
as he cruises down 4th Street and sticks his arm out the window and
    begins to feel
free again
his certainty unchallenged
James Dean was not homosexual
Mark Twain did not have a split personality
Charles Bukowski was not a drunken lout
Frank *could* have been a great blues harmonica player
or a tightrope walker
or a ballet dancer
or ridden the rails back and forth across the country without
getting the shit beat out of him
and as he rolls through green light after green light at 5:21 a.m. Frank
    grins
with that old bachelor-who-can-think-and-do-anything feeling
until
he remembers how lonely it was to come home to Jim Morrison
and Marlon Brando and Vincent van Gogh
and Charles Bukowski every night
people on records and video cassettes and in books who had no idea
who Frank was
people who puked into pianos and punched holes in the wall and
    pulled out their dicks

➢

and pissed on barroom floors and ate paint
none of whom had long red beautiful curly hair like Jane's
hair Frank could run his hands through
as Jane taught Frank a thing or 2 about how boring it is
to always
be right
and how sexy it is
to be wrong.

One of the Joys of Having a Wife Who's Still Alive

Frank has begun to wonder
if he will regret not having loved Jane enough
after she's dead
if he will wish
he would have worn his red and green plaid Christmas pajama
    bottoms
that matched Jane's red and green plaid Christmas pajama bottoms
like she'd wanted him to
when they went to see their 1-year old great-grandson William
just flown over from England for Christmas
instead of feeling like it was too silly and sentimental a thing
for a poet who'd published 3 volumes of his poetry
to do
maybe he'll take out those red and green plaid Christmas pajama
    bottoms
as the dirt settles over Jane's coffin
and hold them grief-stricken
and wish he would have learned to dance
to Frank Sinatra records with Jane like she'd always wanted him to
on those balconies of those inns on all their vacations
in San Francisco
instead of feeling like dancing to Frank Sinatra was something
a tough-as-nails 30-year-veteran machinist
just shouldn't do
and it will be too late
and he will put on one of their old Frank Sinatra records and bury his
    face
in his red and green plaid Christmas pajama bottoms
and weep
as the crows walk across Jane's grave
at 7 am

Maybe,
but as Frank looks over at Jane next to him in bed this Saturday
    morning
he leans over and kisses the beautiful hair on her sleeping head
and smiles

One of the joys of having a wife who's still alive➤

is not having to wear matching red and green Christmas pajama
   bottoms
or dance to Frank Sinatra.

Saint Frank

"What do you mean you wouldn't want to be poet laureate of The
    United States?"
Jane asks Frank as they sip tea in bed Sunday morning
"I wouldn't want to have to suck up to an establishment
that condones continuous austere cutbacks
to The National Endowment for the Arts,"
Frank says proudly
lifting his nose in the air and sticking out his jaw like the man
who won't give information even under threat of being tortured to
    death
"But you'd be getting an endowment to *your* art
Poet laureates get stipends
They get grants and reading fees and you'd get flown all over for free
and be feted and honored and represent your country
and you'd sell hundreds and hundreds of your books!"
Frank shakes his head
and looks stubbornly at his pair of blue work jeans folded over the
    chair and the hole
worn through one of its knees
like a badge of honor
"I wouldn't want to sell out"
Frank smiles proud of himself
like the last cop on a police force who can't be bribed
even though the rest of the cops threaten to cut his balls off
"I wouldn't want to represent a conservative academic establishment
that disrespects accessible narrative poetry"
"Whatta you mean Frank?
You just take the stipends
You just set your ideals aside for a bit and take the stipends
and then later bring your ideals back out again!" Jane says
looking over at Frank
so happy a million miles away rubbing shoulders with Galileo
and Socrates and Sir Thomas More and all the other heroes and
    martyrs and saints
who've given up their freedom or their head or their life
for an ideal
"Okay Frank, drink your tea and have a good time with your petty
    uptight recalcitrance,"
Jane says
    ➢

261

as Frank smiles with self-satisfaction

After all,
no award is better for a man to turn down out of a sense of honor
than one he stands almost no chance
of winning.

Sir Gawain Takes Out the Trash

Frank with Jane
and home from the grueling steel-bending-and-chewing machine shop
    Friday night
wants to celebrate his victory over yet another manhood-testing
week of work
and opens *Sir Gawain and the Green Knight*
reading it aloud to Jane
as a fair lady of the castle tells Sir Gawain,
"You are known as the noblest knight of your age,"
and Frank tells Jane how important courtesy was to Sir Gawain.
"Oh," Jane says,
"You mean like the way you
let the door slam in my face when we're going into a restaurant . . ."
Frank frowns
but continues to read aloud as Sir Gawain
puts on his armor and helmet and picks up his sword with gold-gilded
    hilt
and mounts his noble horse Gringolet.
"Ah," says Jane,
"Just the way you put on your jeans and T-shirt and steel-toed boots
    and pick up
your lunch pail and brave freeway traffic jams
driving to work in your Toyota . . ."
and Frank reads on and Sir Gawain leaves the castle
to ride through the medieval English woods where wild boar and
    wolves roam
to find the Green Chapel
in the wild rocky valley and face the fearsome Green Knight
and test
his New Year's Eve oath by letting the Green Knight strike him a blow
across his neck with a might axe.
"Oh," Jane says
"Well, I cut up some stinky fish today.
On your way to the Green Chapel,
could you please take out the trash?"
Frank rises nobly
and closes *Sir Gawain and the Green Knight*
➤

and goes into the kitchen and grabs the trash and heads out their
    apartment door
and treks down into the wild rocky medieval English valley
of the cracked asphalt Long Beach alley full of thrown-out mattresses
and faces down the terror of the black trash dumpster
the way Sir Gawain laid his neck under the Green Knight's axe
and throws out the stinky fish
and quotes the ending to *Sir Gawain and the Green Knight*:
"Now that man who wore a crown of thorns
he brings us to his bliss! Amen,"
brushing off his hands
triumphant
in his trash can quest
as the Green Knight tells him,
"You are the most faultless man
that ever walked the earth."

Solidarity in Hard Times

One Sunday morning when Frank and Jane are having tea and Frank
   is feeling
especially noble recalling his days in the steel mill he says,
"I used to shove 30 tons of steel a week
into the mouth of a white-hot blast furnace . . ."
waiting for Jane to nod in awe
and sympathy but Jane recalling her days in the go-go bars says,
"I used to carry 4 pitchers of beer in each hand
all night serving the drunks . . ."
"The 2-ton drop hammers used to smash down on the concrete floor
   so hard
it quaked like an earthquake and I could barely walk and my stomach
   rose
and my heart leaped . . ."
Frank goes on
waiting for Jane to realize the immense ordeal he has endured and
   survived
but Jane says, "My legs were so tired after serving beer and go-go
   dancing
for 10 hours with no break
I had to crawl up the stairs to my bedroom at the end of the night . . ."
Frank grips his teacup as hard as a sledgehammer and sticks out his jaw
   and says,
"The drills and the air compressors and the furnaces and the drop
   hammers
were so loud men who worked that steel mill 20 years shook constantly
in their fingers and jaws . . ."
but Jane fires back,
"Those rock bands were so loud I couldn't hear for an hour
after I left work."
Frank is about to slam his teacup down when he stops
and realizes
Jane's bosses screamed at her just as much as his bosses ever screamed
   at him
he realizes
he's been stared at by drugged-out knife-carrying biker machinists
but Jane had drunken crazy men leer and flirt with her bikini fringe
for years
   ➤

he can't win
and Frank gives up and moves over in bed
and snuggles up to Jane and puts his arm around her
while contentedly sipping hot Earl Grey tea and says,
"We've had it pretty rough,"
and smiles.
In America the unions might be busted
and socialism a dirty word
but at least Frank gets to be married
to a beautiful
comrade in arms.

Spark Spent: Mild-Mannered Machinist

"Spark Spent"
Jane calls Frank
referring to the tired shy so-average-he's-boring-never-reads-or-writes-
    anything persona
Frank adopts in the machine shop
Clark Kent who rips off his dorky reporter clothes in that phone booth
to reveal the big "S" for Superman
on his chest
while Frank as Spark Spent comes home
from the machine shop to take off his stinky style-less kryptonite-
    stained shirt and greasy jeans
and reveals on his chest
the big "P"
for Poet Man
then takes a volume of Neruda or Whitman or Akhmatova or
    Shakespeare or Bukowski
off his shelf and throws it open and reads
poetry no one in the machine shop ever dreamed of
and takes pen
and sits down with soul as big as all the stars in the universe to write
a sizzling poem
Frank smiles
as the teeth on the cutter in his machine head make a block of heat-
    treated steel
shudder and smoke
contemplating how boring and uninteresting everyone in this machine
    shop thinks he is
because he has fooled them again with his mild mannered hugs-close-
    to-his-machine-all-day-never-has-anything-to-say
Spark Spent act
as Jane
waits at home for him to burst through the door
and fly with his imagination about the room on the wings of
    inspiration writing
his latest poem
that might change the world
as Poet Man
able to leap tall bookcases in a single bound
➤

faster than a speeding metaphor
more powerful than a locomotive of stream of consciousness
up up and away
for Truth, Justice
and the Poetic Way.

Wasn't Columbus a Bachelor?

"If I had a couple million dollars I'd buy us tickets to outer space!"
Frank says
looking far out with sparkling eyes across the sea to the moon over the horizon
as he and Jane walk the boardwalk in Long Beach
"What?!" Jane says
"You know. That billionaire that's building a shuttle that will take a person
to outer space for a quarter million dollars
I'd buy 2 tickets!"
"Why?!"
"Why?" Frank throws his arm out toward the horizon Columbus sailed into
"Because you fly out past the atmosphere and you're in outer space!
You experience weightlessness
You float around like those people in that movie 2001
and then you look out a window and see the earth
so far away it's curved!"
"I don't like that movie," Jane says
"Outer space is boring. There's nothing there"
"But what an experience! What an adventure!
Wouldn't you like to defy gravity
and look back at the earth floating in the blackness of outer space like a ball?"
"Weightlessness? Defying gravity? How would we pee?
We women would have to be catheterized
You men would have a little cup in your space suit"
"But what about the spectacular view of the curved green earth out the window?
What about the beautiful sunrise?"
"But what about the glare?
They wouldn't let me wear my sunglasses
I'd get a migraine"
"But what about floating weightless
and leaving all your earthbound chains behind?"
"O.K. Carl Sagan! What would we eat?
Suck Spam out of a tube?
We couldn't drink any champagne or cognac
It would float away and get in my hair
➢

269

and make it frizz!"
Frank looks up at the moon over the horizon again and tries to
    concentrate
on the magic of the universe
and floating carefree and weightless in outer space while gazing back
at the green earth's beautiful curved edge
and looks at Jane walking beside him happy with her feet
firmly on the earth

Wasn't Columbus a bachelor?

ABOUT THE AUTHORS

JOHN BRANTINGHAM's poetry and fiction have been published in hundreds of magazines and venues, including Garrison Keillor's *Writer's Almanac, Pearl, Tears in the Fence, Confrontation,* and *The Journal.* His books include *East of Los Angeles* and *Let Us All Pray to Our Own Strange Gods* (forthcoming from World Parade Books). He works at Mt. San Antonio College, where he teaches English and directs the creative writing programs.

KIRSTEN DIERKING's third book of poems, *Tether*, was released by Spout Press in June 2013. She is the author of two previous books of poetry, *Northern Oracle* (Spout Press, 2007) and *One Red Eye* (Holy Cow! Press, 2001). Her poems have been heard on *The Writer's Almanac* and have appeared in numerous journals and anthologies, including Garrison Keillor's *Good Poems, American Places* and *To Sing Along the Way: Minnesota Women Poets from Pre-Territorial Days to the Present.* She is the recipient of a 2010 McKnight Artist Fellowship, a Minnesota State Arts Board Grant for literature, a Loft Literary Center Career Initiative Grant, a SASE/Jerome Grant, and a writing residency at the Banfill-Locke Center for the Arts. She teaches humanities courses at Anoka-Ramsey Community College.

PAUL FERICANO was a finalist in the Alfred Jarry Foundation's 2013 *Cy Schindell Imaginary Book Prize* competition for his notion of a manuscript based on an idea inspired by a Jorie Graham acceptance speech. He was a semifinalist for the 2012 *Casaba Melon Poetry Award* and has been nominated fifty-six consecutive times for a *Pushcart Prize*, tying Joe DiMaggio's major league record. In 1982, he became the first American poet to enter and leave the U.S. Witness Protection Program. www.sinatrasinatra.com.

CHRIS FORHAN, born and raised in Seattle, Washington, is the author, most recently, of the chapbook *Ransack and Dance* (Silver Birch Press, 2013). His other books include *Black Leapt In*, winner of the Barrow Street Press Poetry Prize; *The Actual Moon, The Actual Stars,* winner of the Morse Poetry Prize and a Washington State Book Award; and *Forgive Us Our Happiness*, winner of the Bakeless Prize. His poems have appeared in *Poetry, Paris Review, Ploughshares, New England Review, Parnassus,* and other magazines, as well as in *The Best American Poetry.* He has won a National Endowment for the Arts Fellowship and two Pushcart Prizes and has been a resident at Yaddo and a fellow at Bread Loaf. He lives with his wife, the poet Alessandra Lynch, and their two sons, Milo and Oliver, in Indianapolis, where he teaches at Butler University.

JEFFREY GRAESSLEY lives in La Puente, California. His poems can be found in *Emerge Literary Journal*, *RCC MUSE Magazine*, and the Silver Birch Press *Summer Anthology* (2013). His chapbook *Cabaret of Remembrance* was published by Sweatshoppe Publications in 2013.

DONNA HILBERT'S latest book is *The Congress of Luminous Bodies*, from Aortic Books. *The Green Season*, World Parade Books, a collection of poems, stories and essays, is now available in an expanded second edition. Hilbert appears in and her poetry is the text of the documentary *Grief Becomes Me: A Love Story*, a Christine Fugate film. Earlier books include *Mansions* and *Deep Red*, from Event Horizon, *Transforming Matter* and *Traveler in Paradise* from PEARL Editions and the short story collection *Women Who Make Money and the Men Who Love Them* from Staple First Editions and published in England. Poems in Italian can be found in Bloc notes 59 and in French in *La page blanche*, in both cases, translated by Mariacristina Natalia Bertoli. New work is in recent or forthcoming issues of *5AM*, *Nerve Cowboy*, *PEARL*, *RC Muse*, *Serving House Journal*, *Poets & Artists* and *California Quarterly*. She is a frequent contributor to the online journal *Your Daily Poem*. Her work is widely anthologized, most recently in *The Widows' Handbook*, Kent State University Press. Learn more at donnahilbert.com.

RUTH MOON KEMPHER, an ex-navy brat, and ex-navy wife, was born in Red Bank, New Jersey, many years ago. Her poetry and short prose—fiction and critical articles—have appeared in journals and other periodical publications since verse publications in the early 1960s. In 2012, she won the Bright Hills Press publication competition, and *What I Can Tell You*, the prize winner, was published in 2013. She is now retired from owning The White Lion Tavern in the historic San Agustin Antigua area of St. Augustine, Florida, and from twenty-one years of teaching in the English Department of St. Johns River State College. Since 1994, she has published the work of many poets through her Kings Estate Press, in single chapbooks and anthologies—collections that are always illustrated. After years of living at the beach, she now lives in pine woods in an old cracker house, keeping house for two dogs—Sadie, a long-legged hound, and Mister Frost, an emotional American Husky.

STEVEN KUHN is a poet and photographer who was born in Southern California but quickly relocated to Memphis, Tennessee, where he grew up and still resides with his wife and two cats. He teaches English for Shelby County Schools, brewing his own beer, traveling as much as possible, and maintaining his lifelong love of language. He has been featured in *The Bat Shat* poetry magazine. the Silver Birch Press *Green Anthology*, and the Silver Birch Press *Summer Anthology*, and was recently selected as one of five finalists for Chicago's *Naked Girls Reading* Literary Honors award. Follow his ramblings at steven-kuhn.blogspot.com or on Twitter @StevenKuhnPoet.

TAMARA MADISON teaches English and French at a public high school in Los Angeles. Raised on a citrus farm in the California desert, Tamara's life has taken her many places, including Europe and the former Soviet Union, where she spent fifteen months in the 1970s. A swimmer and dog lover, Tamara says, "All I ever wanted to do with my life was write, and I mostly write poetry because it suits my lifestyle. I like the way one can say so much in the economical space of a poem."

CATFISH MCDARIS has been published widely—in *The Louisiana Review*, *George Mason University Press*, and *New Coin* from Rhodes University in South Africa. He's recently been translated into French, Polish, Swedish, Arabic, Bengali, Tagalog, and Esperanto. His twenty-five years of published material is in the Special Archives Collection at Marquette University in Milwaukee, Wisconsin.

CAROLYN MILLER is a poet and painter living in San Francisco. *Light, Moving*, her most recent book of poetry, was published by Sixteen Rivers Press in 2009, and her first full-length collection, *After Cocteau*, was published by the same press in 2002. Her work has appeared in *The Georgia Review*, *The Southern Review*, and *The Gettysburg Review*, among other journals, and her awards include the James Boatwright III Prize for Poetry from *Shenandoah*, and the Rainmaker Award from *Zone 3*.

JOAN JOBE SMITH, founding editor of *Pearl* and *Bukowski Review*, worked for seven years as a go-go dancer before receiving her BA from CSULB and MFA from University of California, Irvine. A Pushcart Honoree, her award-winning work has appeared internationally in more than five hundred publications, including *Outlaw Bible*, *Ambit*, *Beat Scene*, *Wormwood Review*, and *Nerve Cowboy*—and she has published twenty collections, including *Jehovah Jukebox* (Event Horizon Press, US) and *The Pow Wow Cafe* (The Poetry Business, UK), a finalist for the UK 1999 Forward Prize. In July 2012, with her husband, poet Fred Voss, she did her sixth reading tour of England (debuting at the 1991 Aldeburgh Poetry Festival), featured at the Humber Mouth Literature Festival in Hull. She is the author of the literary memoir *Charles Bukowski Epic Glottis: His Art & His Women (& me)* (Silver Birch Press, 2012). Her writing is featured in *LADYLAND*, an anthology of writing by American women (13e note Éditions, Paris, 2014). Her poem "Uncle

Ray on New Year's Day . . ." [included in this collection] won the 2012 *Philadelphia Poets* John Petracca Prize.

RICK SMITH is a clinical psychologist specializing in domestic violence and brain damage in private practice in Rancho Cucamonga, California. He plays harmonica and writes for The Mescal Sheiks and for Music Formula. He can also heard on CD and vinyl as well as on the soundtrack for Oscar nominee, *Days of Heaven*. His poems have appeared widely and his books include *Exhibition Game* (G. Sack Press, 1973), *The Wren Notebook* (Lummox Press, 2000), *Hard Landing* (Lummox Press, 2010), and *Whispering In A Mad Dog's Ear* (Lummox Press, 2014).

FRED VOSS has been a machinist working in steel mills and factories for thirty-five years. He has published three books of his poetry of the working life with the U.K.'s Bloodaxe Books, the latest of which, *Hammers and Hearts of the Gods*, was named a Book of the Year 2009 by the U.K.'s leading socialist newspaper, *The Morning Star*. His latest collection *Tooth and Fang and Machine Handle* won the 2013 Nerve Cowboy Chapbook competition.

Acknowledgments

John Brantingham
"A Man Stepping into a River": *Serving House Journal* and *The Green of Sunset*
"God Save the Queen": *Askew Magazine* and *The Green of Sunset* (Moon Tide Press, 2013)
"A Sestina about Fathers and Sons and Deserts and the Leonids Meteor Shower and How All Those Things Come Together to Show Us that Dreamers Like Me Absolutely Need Practical People Like My Father and I Try Not to Be Condescending as I Do It, but I Might Fail a Little": *Generationless*
"Sequoia National Park, 1987," "San Dimas 1987," "Summer, 1982," "The Trail to Bearpaw Meadow, Sequoia National Park, 1978," "The Trail to Bearpaw Meadow, Sequoia National Park, 1985," "The Trail to Bearpaw Meadow, Sequoia National Park, 2005," "Starbucks on a Saturday Night, "Stopping in a Target in New York," "Lightning Storm": *The Green of Sunset* (Moon Tide Press, 2013)
"Meditation on a Lightning Storm that Happened in 1894": *The Green of Sunset* (Moon Tide Press, 2013) and *Synesthesia*

Kirsten Dierking
From *Northern Oracle* (Spout Hill Press, 2007) : "Northern Oracle," "Border Lines," "Shoveling Snow," "The Animist."
From *Tether* (Spout Hill Press, 2013): "In Early Evening," "Kayak," "Mississippi," "Deep Winter," "In February," "Think of Mexico," "Lilacs," "Thunder."

Paul Fericano
Magazines and Online Journals: *The Broadsider, The Bubble, The Dust Congress, Four By Two, Haggard and Halloo, Medusa's Kitchen, Minestrone, The Outlaw Poetry Network, Poems For All, Star West, The Wormwood Review.*
Collections: *Commercial Break*, Paul Fericano (Poor Souls Press, 1982). *Loading the Revolver with Real Bullets*, Paul Fericano (Second Coming Press, 1977).
Anthologies: *A Bird Black as the Sun* (Green Poet Press, 2011), *But Buddy I'm a Kind of Poem: A Sinatra Anthology* (Entasis Press, 2008), *Italo-American Poets, a Bilingual Anthology* (Carello Editore, 1985).

Chris Forhan
"Aspirin and Shadow": *Pleiades*
"Bone Box:": *Image*
"Crude Articulation": *The Georgia Review*
"Dream: Obedience": *The Laurel Review*
"Industrial Gothic": *Cerise Press*
"The Mother of Beauty": *The Broome Review*
"Nothing to It": *New Orleans Review*

"Petition" and "While Reading The Lives of the Saints in a Lawn Chair":
   The Recorder: Journal of the American Irish Historical Society
"Tattletale" and "Third Grade": *Prairie Schooner*

JEFFREY GRAESSLEY
"I Can Hear An Angel Singing": *Rusty Nail Magazine*
"Dark Brown Hair": *Gutter Eloquence Magazine*
"Empty Hours": Silver Birch Press *Summer Anthology*

DONNA HILBERT
"The Doctor Book," "Mother in Satin," "Queens": *Deep Red* (Event Horizon, 1993)
"1942 Snapshot of my Father," "In Plowboy's Produce Market," "Mansions": *Mansions* (Event Horizon, 1990)
"Craving," "City of Lakewood," "Grief Becomes Me," "Lesson": (*Transforming Matter*, PEARL Editions, 2000)
"Madeleine," "Domestic Arts," "Joined," "Credo," "What God Wants": *The Green Season*, 2nd edition (World Parade Books, 2008)
"In the First Years," "Deshacer," "The Angel Garmin": *The Congress of Luminous Bodies*, (Aortic Books, 2013)
"Traveler," "Flowers": *Traveler in Paradise* (PEARL Editions, 2004)

RUTH MOON KEMPHER
"Rutabagas": *Alpha Beat*
"Tongues": *Bogg*
"Patience, I Tell Myself": *Confrontation*
"Driving Home on Beach Road": *Front Window*
"Toenail": *Kalliope*
"Arrangement, with Tiger Lilies": *Presa*
"Fortune Teller" and "Hands: Home After Bowling": *Tiger's Eye*
"Conjure Lines—Sea Changes": *Waterways*
"Hazy at the Market": *Wormwood Review*

STEVE KUHN
"Word": *The Bat Shat*

TAMARA MADISON
"Sweet Potato": *SpotLit*
"Missing Whom": Bank Heavy Press
"To a Mortar": *East Jasmine Review*
"Cocktail Party": *Nerve Cowboy*

CAROLYN MILLER
"In the Garden," "Community Garden," "Garden in Late Winter," "Rose Garden, Summer Solstice": *Light, Moving* (Sixteen Rivers Press, 2009).
"Susan's Garden": *This Is Mine* (Protean Press, 2004).
"City Garden": *Constant Lover* (Protean Press, 2001).

RICK SMITH
Some poems previously appeared in *Amoskeag, Aspect, Chaffey Review, Comstock Review, Familiar; Hanging Loose, Lummox Journal, Malpais Review, paperplates, Parent's Blessing, Penumbra, Pinyon, Rockbottom, Rockhurst Review, Say It At My Wedding,* Silver Birch Press *Summer Anthology, Spillway,* and *Unwound.*
"By Love Joined": *Exhibition Game* (G. Sack Press, 1973).
"Hands That Hold": *Whispering In A Mad Dog's Ear* (Lummox Press, 2014).

JOAN JOBE SMITH
"Deep in the Heart of Texas." "More Secrets About Beans": *Wormwood Review*
"Peach Tree Santa Claus," "The Red River,": *Nerve Cowboy*
"Born Not to Laugh at Tornadoes": *The Pow Wow Café* (UK)
"The French're Different from Me and You": *The Bastille* (Paris, France)
"Uncle Ray Calls New Year's Day . . .": *Philadelphia Poets* (Winner of 2012 John Petracca Poetry Prize)

FRED VOSS
"Sir Gawain Takes Out the Trash": *Ambit* (UK)
"Comrades in Arms": *Dwang:* 2014
"Absent-Minded Poet Laureate Garbage Man": *Chiron Review*
"Frank Almost Writes His First Poem About Paris": *The Bastille* (Paris, France)

www.ingramcontent.com/pod-product-compliance
Lightning Source LLC
Chambersburg PA
CBHW070547050426
42450CB00011B/2753